FRAUD

Copyright © 2017 by Istoria Ministries

All rights reserved. This book or any portion thereof may not be reproduced or used in any manner whatsoever without the express written permission of the publisher except for the use of brief quotations in a book review.

Printed in the United States of America

First Printing, 2017

ISBN: 978-1-52032344-2

Istoria Ministries
1112 W. York
Enid, Oklahoma 73703

www.istoriaministries.com
www.wadeburleson.org

FRAUDULENT AUTHORITY

Contents

Acknowledgments (p. 4)

Foreword: There's Only One Authority in the Church (p. 7)

Chapter 1: The Church Is Losing Transforming Power (p. 11)

Chapter 2: The Infatuation with Church Authority (p. 16)

Chapter 3: The Institutional Church Isn't Jesus (p. 21)

Chapter 4: The Problem with Church Authority (p. 24)

Chapter 5: All Authority Is Christ's Alone (p. 27)

Chapter 6: No Office of Authority for Either Pastors or Deacons (p. 30)

Chapter 7: Nobody Rules Over Anyone Else (p. 35)

Chapter 8: Real Authority in the Church (p. 40)

Chapter 9: It Takes a Covenant to Raise a Bitter Root (p. 45)

Chapter 10: Five Reasons to Say No to a Covenant (p. 51)

Chapter 11: Authority in the New Testament (p. 57)

Chapter 12: Who Is the Boss at Your Church? (p. 62)

Chapter 13: Ordination Is the Mother of Authority (p. 66)

Chapter 14: Service to Others without Authority Over (p. 70)

Chapter 15: Illustrating Anointed Female Ministry (p. 77)

Chapter 16: Gifted Women Are Wrongly Excluded (p. 80)

Chapter 17: Moving Away from Male Authority (p. 85)

Chapter 18: The Bizarre Practices of Male Authority (p. 100)

Chapter 19: Only "That" Woman Should Be Quiet (p. 105)

Chapter 20: The Misinterpretation of I Timothy 2:9-15 that Leads to Male Authority (p. 120)

Chapter 21: All the Ekklesia Have Voices (p. 131)

Chapter 22: Do You Think of a Building with a Steeple or a Body of People? (p. 137)

Chapter 23: A Word about "Authority" in Marriage (p. 140)

Chapter 24: The Divorce Rate and Men Who Have Authority in Marriage (p. 145)

Chapter 25: A Warning to Those Who Rule Over Others for Material Gain (p. 156)

Afterword: A Healthy Church (p. 167)

A Request from the Author (p. 174)

Acknowledgments

It's been my privilege to be the pastor of a remarkable church in northwest Oklahoma since 1992. The people of Emmanuel Enid have been a blessing to my family and me in more ways than I can count.

Emmanuel Enid has never attempted to take away my freedom to articulate biblical principles that often seem to run contrary to accepted church culture. Like the Bereans, the people of Emmanuel have "searched the Scriptures" to see whether what their pastor is saying is true.

The members have been willing to end cherished church traditions that brought praise and applause to the people of Emmanuel, a decision based solely on answering the question *"Will our ministries advance the Kingdom of Christ or are they designed to make us feel better about ourselves?"*

In other words, are lives being transformed by the power of the Spirit through what we do through our church body? For some, giving up cherished traditions is not easy, particularly when those traditions give a sense of comfort and identity to the people involved.

When the people of Emmanuel Enid decided to end certain church ministries or religious traditions because they no longer reach people for Christ or advance His Kingdom, some members disagreed. But everyone understood they were loved and accepted as a valuable part of Emmanuel Enid, even in disagreement.

That's the ultimate test of unity.

FRAUDULENT AUTHORITY

The absence of disagreement is not unity; the presence of love in the midst of disagreement is.

The ability to separate the business of the 501C-3 non-profit called Emmanuel Baptist Church, Enid, Oklahoma from Kingdom work is tangible among the leadership at Emmanuel.

The state requires bylaws, trustees, pastors, etc., but these legal requirements are never confused for Kingdom work. Refusing to spiritualize state standards is a blessing that not many churches experience or even understand. The people of Emmanuel Enid do.

Therefore, business decisions are never couched as "the will of God," but are open for debate, for the admission of mistakes, and ultimate rest in the Providence of God.

I want to acknowledge the contribution of four remarkable people, three men, and one woman.

First, my wife, Dr. Rachelle Burleson is the smartest, prettiest, classiest, kindest, and most grace-filled person I know. She makes life fun for me.

Second, the three men are remarkable theologians and writers in their own right. Paul Burleson, my father, has taught me more about ministry than all others else combined. He writes the Foreword.

Chuck Andrews, a friend and deeply intellectual pastor, has written the Afterword which summarizes what a church should look like when authority is properly understood.

FRAUDULENT AUTHORITY

Fob James, a lawyer from Alabama with a keen understanding of authority in the Bible, has written extensively on the subject and has permitted me to publish an article of his that I found convincing. These three men help me understand I'm not alone on an island of thought.

Finally, I would like to acknowledge those of you who have suffered under horrible spiritual abuse and didn't know how to get out from under it. I could write story after story of people who've written to me about their trauma of abuse by authoritarian pastors who act as if they are God's vicar on earth. Some pastors seek to control – and sometimes punish – those who oppose God and God's "ordained authority" on earth, or otherwise known as "the pastor."

You know your story.

I tell just a couple of stories in this book. My greater purpose is to help you understand how to come out from under abusive spiritual authority, recognizing it as the opposite of biblical Christianity.

For all you who love the Bible and God but question the pastor and the rules of the church, I hope you read and understand *Fraudulent Authority* so that you can escape spiritual church abuse with clear biblical thinking and a heart filled with grace and understanding of what Christ's Church should be.

May God ever keep us aware of, and away from, *Fraudulent Authority*.

Wade Burleson
January 2017

Foreword: There's Only One Authority in the Church

Authority in a local church is a much debated and, as I've discovered of late, a much-misunderstood concept. Having served as a pastor for nearly six decades, I know firsthand the ease in which a pastor can assume "rule over" or "control over" the lives of other people.

It's never easy to resist a form of control that comes in the name of God, but *Fraudulent Authority* will help you consider whether or not the pastor or church leader with whom you serve wrongly believes he "rules over" you and other people he is leading. There are a few basic principles which serve as the foundation for all you will read in the chapters to come.

Principle 1: There is only one head of the Church/churches, and all authority is His.

If anyone ever assumes authority because of their person or position they are usurping the authority of the Head (Ephesians 4:5,15).

Principle 2: The Head of the Body has given an authoritative Word to the members of the Body (universal and local).

The Old and New Testaments are that inspired Word. New Covenant people are bound to the New Testament writings (Hebrews 1:2, Acts 18:28).

Principle 3: All believers are responsible to the Head individually and have a responsibility to each other (Romans 14:4, Ephesians 5:21).

FRAUDULENT AUTHORITY

All believers are priests unto God and are gifted by God. Therefore, all must take their place among the body members to minister for the good of all (1 Corinthians 12-14).

Principle 4: There are certain ones [both men and women] who are gifted as all members are, but, then become a gift to the body in a unique way.

The purpose of these people/gifts is to equip all for ministry (Ephesians 4:11-12).

Principle 5: There is no emphasis in the New Testament on "authority" derived from an "office."

The King James Version translates the word "office" in Rom. 11:13, 12:4, and 1Tim 3:1. But in Rom. 11:13 it is the word "*diakonia*" or "service." In 12:4 it is "praxis" which means "action" or "function." In I Timothy 3:1 the word "office" is not in the original text at all. The verse says in the original "if anyone aspires to oversight [*episkope*]"

There is no "office" of authority in the church of Jesus Christ.

Leadership is experienced in the assembly because the gifts and ministries of the Holy Spirit are obvious in and through people of good character who persuade by their example. In one sense, the entire body shares authority (Ephesians 5:21, 1 Peter 5:5).

Followers of Jesus recognize one another's gifts, knowledge, and experiences in the Lord, and we *choose* to serve or follow leaders because the Holy Spirit has placed these gifted and older people in the assembly as gifts to us. That is the key to understanding Pastors/Elders and their function. No one has authority because they have a stronger personality, knows more Bible, or they hold an office.

That is foreign to the New Testament. Paul the Apostle had to defend his Apostleship by it being the work of the Spirit setting him aside for it. 1 Timothy 5:17 speaks of those Elders that "give oversight well"...."are worthy of double honor."

It is the ability "give oversight well" that is the source of their leadership. This ability is defined as Holy Spirit anointing. In other words, the anointing of the Spirit makes clear the authority that rests on a ministry done well, not the office holder's position of authority or any inherent authority within an office, because there is no authority like this in the church.

These principles will be expanded upon in the coming chapters. As you read, you may be led to some new conclusions about church leadership, church ministry, and so-called pastoral authority. For example:

1). Churches built around a "one-man show" are foreign to the New Testament.

2). Submission to authority is given to those who "serve" the body well, whatever area of "service" that might be and regardless of "gender."

Some people believe that the Spirit will never place a woman functioning as a shepherd, teacher, or encourager (the role of a pastor). Whether that is true or not, "authority" and "submission" are never "gender-based" in the New Covenant, but are rather "Holy Spirit ministry" based, for the Spirit gifts His people as He sees fit. No one is to be a leader

FRAUDULENT AUTHORITY

by saying "I'm the Pastor/Elder" or "I have a Seminary degree" or "I'm a man."

3). Servanthood is the "badge" of Christian living and is to be the overriding characteristic of body-life. If God's people are ever to reflect the biblical relationship of the Head (Christ) to the members (us), then servanthood is essential.

4). The rule of church life is to be the Headship of Christ, the priesthood of all believers, and each member contributing with giftedness and edifying each other in the process. There is biblical freedom for a gathering of believers to set up any system, any format, any procedure to carry out business, but each church body is to function under the anointing of the Spirit, serving one another.

5). A church or church leaders that understand Christ's authority and the spiritual gifts of all those in Christ will respect all Christians, be open and receptive to any disagreement from other believers, and will never subvert the Lordship of Christ by seeking to "rule over" other Christians.

These outcomes must be practice, not just theory, in a church that desires the reality of Christ to a lost world in need of the gospel. Check any church leadership by these standards if you want to be biblical in church life.

Fraudulent Authority will help you understand the biblical reason to live your life and lead your church with an acknowledgment that Jesus Christ alone rules over His people.

Chapter 1: The Church Is Losing Its Transforming Power

The church of Jesus Christ in the 21st century is losing its power to transform lives because of an *infatuation with the spiritual and moral authority that pastors take over people.*

Authoritarianism in the church has become the biggest challenge Christians face in the 21st century.

So-called "spiritual authority" in leaders who demand people submit to their will and ways in the name of God, is tearing at the fabric of legitimate New Covenant Christianity.

Church leaders present themselves as the vicars of God, spokespersons for the Spirit of God, and the human embodiment of Divine truth. This fraudulent spiritual authority—the basis for Christian leaders "ruling over" other Christians--permeates much of the modern evangelical church structure.

Christians cross or go against this fraudulent spiritual authority at their peril.

Authoritarian leaders in the church have a unique form of punishment.

One will never feel more isolated and alone than when a pastor calls down the wrath of God upon a church member who dares question his leadership.

FRAUDULENT AUTHORITY

The world has established systems of governance using imperial forms of authority, but the church is not supposed to imitate the world. We are to be in it, but not of it.

Webster's defines authority as *"the power to influence thought, opinion, or behavior by **convincing force or control**."*

Governments have authority. Kings have authority. Presidents have authority. Leadership in these systems of governance comes from those sitting in *positions of authority.*

The church of Jesus Christ was never designed to operate in this manner.

Jesus explicitly taught in Matthew 23:8-11 that the only person who rules over Christian communities is the Lord. He is our Teacher. He is our Leader. He is our Instructor.

Under Him, we are all brothers. We are all equals.

Jesus told us that the world's system of top-down governance should not exist among His people.

Listen to our Lord's words:

"Those who have recognized as rulers of the Gentiles lord their positions over the people; and their great men exercise authority over them. *But it is not to be this way among you*, for whoever wishes to become great among you shall be your servant" (Mark 10:42-43).

Jesus often said to those who followed Him, *"**The greatest among you shall be your servant**"* (Matthew 23:11).

FRAUDULENT AUTHORITY

There was no emphasis in Jesus' teaching or the New Testament letters on any alleged authority that is derived from any "office" or position.

Let me repeat that:

Nowhere in the New Testament does it say that a Christian, because of title or position, has moral authority over another Christian.

There is no "office of authority" or position of authority in the body of Christ like there is an office of President of the United States. Christ alone has and holds the only position of authority within His Church, and He has no vicar on earth but His Spirit, who resides in the life of every believer.

Christians are to serve others, and any leadership of any Christian gathering flows from this selfless service. Pagans seek offices that grant authority so that their leadership (lordship) over other people is inherent to their positions or titles.

Christians are to persuade others about morality by our love and grace; pagans morally coerce others by their positions of authority.

When Christians act like pagans, we turn our homes, churches, and organizations into structures of authority where everybody is coerced to submit to another person's authority, and the control of a person extends from someone else in a higher 'position' of authority rather than Jesus Christ.

The equality of New Covenant believers in Christ is lost because Old Covenant Levitical forms of authority are imposed on Christian ministry.

FRAUDULENT AUTHORITY

How does one know if the Christian community, church or family to which he or she belongs is following Christ's teachings on leadership or is a reflection of the pagan's understanding of authority?

What are the signs of imperial authoritarianism in the church?

The following are ten indicators of Fraudulent Authority within Christian organizations and churches.

1). There is never any freedom to question leaders.

2). Leaders often make claims of having special insights from God, insights that others are unable to possess.

3). Disagreements with leaders are deemed as signs of the devil's influence in one's life.

4). Events are designed to bring attention and praise to leaders rather than equipping others to do the work of the ministry.

5). Any concept of equality is immediately labeled rebellion or the result of "liberal" denials of the Bible.

6). Authoritarian leaders are only comfortable around likeminded leaders; thus, there is an unofficial 'speaking tour' where only imperial, authoritarian leaders share the platform with each other.

7). The measure of success becomes the number of people who follow the leader ("It must be of God! Look at how many come to hear me speak!")

(8). If a person leaves the community or church, the problem is always in the person who leaves, not the leadership.

9). Leaders who wrongly perceive themselves as those "with authority" insulate their lives by demanding absolute loyalty by giving large financial benefits to their closest 'advisors.'

10). The ultimate end of this kind of Christian leadership is always more; more money, more power, more, more, more. The people of Christ are beginning to awaken to abuses of authority in the modern church and home.

This book will help you understand how anyone who seeks to "rule over you" is usurping the role of Christ as Lord and Savior of your life. We are all called to submit to the Lordship of Christ and His authority, not any man's authority.

This book is written to help empower you to Christ alone and refrain from thinking anyone else, but He holds the keys of authority in His Kingdom.

Chapter 2: The Infatuation with Church Authority

I recently received an email from a person who attends the church where Chuck Swindoll serves as Teaching Pastor:

"I attend Chuck Swindoll's church in Frisco, Texas. This past Sunday he indicated that the biblical way to choose Elders is for them to be hand selected by the existing elder board (slowly, carefully, with many investigations and with God's leading). He specifically called out Southern Baptists indicating that the Bible does not sanction congregational voting for elders/deacons and specifically that women cannot be elders. What are your thoughts?"

Here are a few thoughts for my anonymous Internet friend about churches that place men in positions of "authority" over congregations.

(1). The mistake many churches make is spiritualizing the legal and legalizing the spiritual.

A 501C-3 non-profit is a legal corporation. It is not a spiritual entity.

Every state requires a 501C-3 non-profit entity (like churches) to incorporate. On the legal incorporation papers, the "officers" of the non-profit are listed. These individuals-- and only these individuals--are those who have the *legal authority* and carry the *fiduciary responsibility* for that non-profit (according to the state).

FRAUDULENT AUTHORITY

Is Chuck Swindoll saying he believes a woman cannot have this "legal authority?"

Surely not. I'm sure Chuck would argue his wife can have legal authority. Never in Scripture is a woman forbidden from entering into a legal contract, engaging in a commercial activity or obtaining any personal legal authority. Lydia sold purple dye. Phoebe sailed from Cenchrea to Rome on a commercial ship (carrying in the folds of her robe the letter to the Romans).

To say that "only men" can have legal authority (i.e., be officers of a non-profit, whether they are called elders, trustees) is illogical, impractical, and bordering on the absurd.

So what Pastor Chuck seems to be doing is making the mistake of spiritualizing the legal.

What he must be saying is that a woman cannot have *"spiritual authority."* The problem with Swindoll's view is his infatuation with spiritual authority.

He thinks that a woman cannot have spiritual authority **"over a man."** Where he gets this view is an absolute mystery to me, but he is not the only one infected with it.

The problem is not his view of gender; the problem is his view that someone other than Jesus Christ can have spiritual or moral authority over another believer.

The Bible teaches that men and women should be "servants of all" and nobody should seek or desire to have moral or spiritual "authority" over anyone. Evangelical men seem infatuated with obtaining this spiritual authority and

FRAUDULENT AUTHORITY

preventing women from having it. The problem is their infatuation with spiritual authority.

In the New Testament, Jesus Christ is the Head, the sole authority over every single believer regarding spiritual life and moral well-being. Each believer in Jesus Christ (both male and female) is a priest unto God (i.e., "the priesthood of the believer"), modeling for the world what it means to walk with God. Christians serve one another, encourage one another, and help one another, but the moment somebody tries to take a position of spiritual authority over another person he or she has crossed a line in terms of New Testament Christianity.

Again, the mistake Swindoll is making—a mistake that many Christians make—is spiritualizing the legal and legalizing the spiritual.

The state mandates that certain people within a 501C-3 non-profit have legal authority.

But the true church of Jesus Christ is not a 501C-3 non-profit. The church is not a building.

The church is a woman with the Spirit of Christ living in her. The church is a man with the Spirit of Christ living in him. The church is people who love Christ, and the only spiritual authority over those people is Christ Himself. Period.

If some Christians gather together corporately and start a 501C- 3 non-profits, then, of course, there are people given "legal authority" but nowhere does Scripture state females cannot have this authority.

FRAUDULENT AUTHORITY

(2). When a "group of men" hand select those who are to have so-called spiritual authority over the church, then positions of authority in the church are created--an action strictly forbidden by Christ.

The difference between boys and men is the size of their toys.

Boys want to boss neighborhood kids to be seen as "the boss" and having the first choice of all the prizes. Men want to boss adults for the same reason, though the prizes are different (bigger and better). Fighting for authority and control over other people is an activity that ought not to be acceptable among Christians.

Evangelical men should want to serve all and rule over none. It is my view that the #1 problem in the evangelical church does not revolve around gender issues, nor financial issues, nor doctrinal issues. The #1 problem in the evangelical church revolves around the desire of evangelical men to grab hold of spiritual authority in the church. Jesus Christ said the pagans "bestow titles and give positions of authority," but He said to His followers "it shall not be so among you!" (Mark 10:43).

Anywhere there is an attempt to grab authority and positions of spiritual power or hold on to authority and positions of power (re-electing boards of elders by elders choosing elders) then you are in a church where Ichabod may be written across the threshold. Nowhere in the New Testament does it say that a Christian, because of title or position, has moral authority over another Christian.

For those who use the Hebrews 13 passages to support "moral and spiritual authority over other Christians," I would urge you to read further in Fraudulent Authority where this passage is specifically discussed.

(3). A homosexual family is distinctly dysfunctional by having two men serve as mother/father to their children, a parental role designed by God to include both genders. In like manner, an evangelical church that only allows only men in "leadership positions" is as dysfunctional as a homosexual marriage because gifted women have been excluded from leadership.

There is a distinct feel to a church that is infatuated with "male authority." Power, control, a lack of freedom, pride, aggression, deceit, and spiritual abuse are usually present. Functioning in life in a manner that is opposite of the way God designed us is to bring all kinds of pain into the family of God. Churches that allow men to continue in the belief that they have some power or "inherent authority" over women is to continue in an anti- New Covenant and anti-Christ model.

In the New Covenant, Jesus gave to His co-heirs in the Kingdom – regardless whether they are slaves or free, rich or poor, male or female, black or white -- all the riches of His grace. We are equals when it comes to spiritual authority.

Jesus Christ is the Head of His church, and the notion that the church of Jesus Christ should go back to the forms and function of Old Covenant Judaism (e.g., male priests, sanctuary rituals) is totally contrary to the teaching of the New Testament Scriptures.

Chapter 3: The Institutional Church Isn't Jesus, nor Vice Versa

In this book, I will address some common misconceptions about authority in the local church. Spiritual authority in the church is a much talked about issue in our day.

What you believe about "authority" in the church will touch on every area of your life. From how you read the Bible and understand its teaching, to seeking counsel and direction in your life, to almost every area of Christian living, your understanding of authority in the church—what it is, where it comes from, and who has it—affects everything.

Authority in the church has often been misunderstood or misapplied by Christians due *to cultural and personal biases*, basing their views on poor translations of the sacred text, or by wrongly assuming that the Word of God supports religious traditions regarding authority.

When we speak of the church, we must define what we mean.

A legally incorporated business that the state calls "a church" is a *business institution that has individuals who've been given legal authority by the state government to sign documents, buy and sell land, and enter into business contracts.*

 The constitution of the local church identifies those individuals who have this legal authority in the eyes of the state. It is important for every member of a local church to know who bears legal responsibility for their particular church.

FRAUDULENT AUTHORITY

However, if the state were to shut down the church's legal organization, *the living organism that the Bible calls "the church" will continue.*

The Bible defines the church of Jesus Christ as a living body of believers who are wed to Christ. The purpose of this book is to answer the following question biblically.

Who has spiritual authority *over* believers in the church?

The biblical answer will be clear: Jesus Christ alone has spiritual authority over His people.

Tangentially, other questions need to be answered:

Who can teach others within the church about Jesus Christ and assist people to grow stronger through faith in Him?

Who can help others to deepen their satisfaction and joy in Jesus Christ? Who can lead church committees to conduct the work of Christ's kingdom?

Who can evangelize, baptize, and disciple people in need of faith in Jesus Christ?

Who can give counsel and guidance in the church to help others look to Jesus Christ as the Source of real life and as the one true Authority over all of life?

The biblical answer to these questions is clear:

Those whom God has gifted, Christ has called, and the Spirit has anointed – regardless of gender, race, socio-economic status, or any assumed title or position within the church – are

FRAUDULENT AUTHORITY

those from whom Christ's authority flows and God's people are strengthened spiritually.

Evangelicals today need of a clear understanding of what the Bible says about "authority in the church," and if our practices conflict with the clear principles of the New Covenant inaugurated by Christ, then we need to attempt to correct our mistaken ideas and practices within the church.

Chapter 4: The Problem with Church Authority

The problem faced by many local churches regarding authority is the traditional and non-biblical practice of giving or recognizing "spiritual authority" because of one's gender, church title, or personal influence within a city or the community at large.

Jesus said that the Gentiles bestow authority with positions of honor, but this is something that His followers should never do. The Greek word for **authority** is exousia. It comes from a verb that means

1). To do something without hindrance, or,
2). The right to do something or the right to be over something.

When someone has authority, it means that they wield influence and lead others in the accomplishment of a purpose.

The world at large operates with titles and positions that have inherent authority and power with those titles and positions. Politics, law enforcement, military organizations, educational institutions, and corporations all bestow power and authority in a hierarchy of leadership positions.

Christ's ways, however, are the opposite of the world's ways. Listen to His words: "Those who are recognized as rulers of the Gentiles lord it over them: and their great men exercise authority over them. But it is not (to be) this way among you. Whoever wishes to become great among you shall be your servant, and whoever wishes to be first among you shall be the slave of all. For even the Son of man did not come to be served, but to serve, and to give His life a ransom for many." (Mark 10:42-45)

An interesting side note is that the Greek word for authority (*exousia*) is used only **one time** in the entire New Testament about Christian marriage. Paul says, "The wife does not have authority over her own body but yields it to her husband. In the same way, the husband does not have authority over his own body but yields it to his wife" (I Corinthians 7:4).

The Scripture clearly states in this verse that the husband and the wife have mutual authority over one another in sexual intercourse.

No Christian husband is ever to take authority over his wife sexually, and vice versa. The consummation of Christian marriage is a mutually *shared* right or privilege between both the husband and the wife. Again, this is the only time the word *exousia* (authority) is used about marriage in the Bible, and it is never used about the local church at all.

More importantly, the belief that the husband has "authority" over his wife is far more pagan than biblical or Christian.

One might ask, "But what about the passages that refer to the husband being the 'head over the wife'?"

The English word "head" (see Ephesians 5:23 and I Corinthians 11:3) comes from a Greek word that is not generally used to convey the concept of authority over anyone.

FRAUDULENT AUTHORITY

It is the Greek word *kephale* (pronounced kef-a-lay) and its most common usage in everyday Greek is that of source or beginnings.

Our English word "head" can convey the meaning of the "source" as well. For example, "the headwaters of a river" means the source or the beginning of a river.

Knowing that *kephale* has a different meaning than *exousia* is important to interpret texts like Ephesians 5:23 and I Corinthians 11:3 properly. In those verses, the word *kephale* is translated into English as "head." I believe head should lead you to think "source of" and not "authority over."

Regardless of how you choose to translate *kephale,* it's evident from other texts in Scripture that there is only one Head (authority) over a person in the Kingdom of Christ, and that Head is Jesus Christ.

FRAUDULENT AUTHORITY

Chapter 5: All Authority Is Christ's Alone

The Greek word *exousia* (authority) is used of Jesus Christ in the Bible several places, including:

1. When He was executing judgment (see John 5:27),
2. When He took authority over His own life in the resurrection (see John 10:18),
3. When He gives eternal life (see John 17:2),
4. When He forgives sins (see Mark 1:22; 9:6 and Luke 5:24)
5. When He heals the sick (see Matthew 9:8), a
6. When He casts out demons (see Mark 1:27).

Jesus Christ is also said in Scripture to have "all authority" (see Matthew 28:18).

Jesus is called the Head over all other authorities (see Colossians 2:10).

The word *exousia* (authority) is used of believers four times:

1. In becoming the sons of God (see John 1:12),
2. When casting out demons (see Matthew 10:1),
3. When ruling with Christ over cities after His return (see Luke 19:17),
4. When having access to the tree of life in Heaven (see Revelation 22:14).

The word *exousia* is also used in owning property (see Acts 5:4), the right to eat food offered to idols (see I Corinthians 8:9-11; translated liberty), and several other places in Scripture.

FRAUDULENT AUTHORITY

However, what is missing in the Bible is any place where *exousia* (authority) is used in relationship to someone having authority over a believer in the context of the church.

Nor is *exousia* (authority) ever used in relation to any alleged office of pastor or deacon. As we will see, the Bible never speaks of offices of power and authority within the church.

The church does have authority, but authority comes from giftings the Lord Jesus Christ gives His people. He has given each of us who comprise His church freedom and liberty to serve others as He gifts us to serve (see I Corinthians 8:9).

We are each free in Christ to follow His leadership and commands in our lives, for He is our authority. In Christ's church, no other human being is to lord over other people. So, the freedom we have in Christ is to be used for the welfare and good of other people, and there is no Christian who is to rule over any other Christian.

Jesus possesses ALL authority. When we exercise the gifts He has given us, fulfill the calling He has placed on us as we live our lives anointed by the Spirit (i.e., the fruit of the Spirit), we will exercise His authority in the church. Christ's authority is based on our sacrificial giving, serving, and humility of character.

Likewise, authority in the church is evidenced as we love, serve, teach, and admonish one another, but *authority in the church never resides in anyone's position in the church.*

While it is true that historically the concept of authority in the church has emphasized the idea of being over others, this idea is a cultural concept and is not a biblical mandate

FRAUDULENT AUTHORITY

at all. Jesus made that crystal clear with His rather stark statement that while the Gentiles exercise rule over others, it is NOT to be that way among believers (Mark 10:43).

There are two false practices in the church that continue to foster the mistaken notion that church authority is being over other people instead of being the greatest servant of all people.

One false practice is the unfortunate division between clergy and laity where the former do the work of ministry, and the latter pay the salary of the former as *professional* ministers. We are not saying that paying someone on a church staff is wrong. What we are saying is that the division between clergy and laity is not biblical.

All believers are called to be ministers, and there are to be no elevated positions of authority and power in the church. Sometimes people will be paid to do the work of the ministry because he or she is devoting full-time attention to the ministry.

The other false practice is for pastors, elders, or deacons to rule over the church because the office of pastor or deacon has an inherent authority within the office. For this reason, some within the church grant authority to the pastor because they believe God has given the pastor greater authority because of his position.

Neither of these concepts is a biblical viewpoint for authority in local church life. The constitution of an institutional church may grant legal authority to a group of elders or deacons, but this is a cultural practice of preference, not a biblical model at all. Again, legal authority is required by the state, but this legal authority has nothing to do with spiritual authority in the church.

Chapter 6: No Office of Authority for Either Pastors or for Deacons

Many churches see the word deacon as conveying the idea of an office that those ordained to that office have authority for the leading of the church. I will use this phrase "office of deacon" to illustrate the unbiblical nature of this concept which we have accepted (unfortunately) as scriptural.

We don't deny that there were those who were set aside *to serve the saints* in the first-century church. Acts 6 shows this as well as other passages.

However, when New Testament believers used the Greek word *diakonia* (we use the English word *deacon*) to describe what was being done within that early congregation, they had in mind the attitude of Jesus who had "made Himself of no reputation and took upon Him the form of a servant..." (Philippians 2:7).

What they had observed in Him was washing human feet, feeding the multitudes, healing the sick, always as one serving, and thus, He left us an example that can only be explained with the Greek word *diakonia* (remember, we say deacon) which means *ministering or serving*.

But there is no hint from Scripture that the early Christians considered *deacons* as having any authority because of "an office" in the church (like the "Office of President of the United States").

The general sense of the word *diakonia* is "to assist," which indicates not just to work in general, but *a work that benefits someone else*. This is true whether it was a ministry of waiting on tables or a ministry of the word.

Diakonia was a serving ministry (Acts 6:2-4).

Paul used the word *diakonos* to describe himself as a servant of the Lord (1 Corinthians 3:5), a servant of God (2 Corinthians 6:4), a servant of the new covenant (2 Corinthians 3:6), a servant of the gospel (Ephesians 3:7, Colossians 1:23) and a servant of the church (Colossians 1:25).

Paul noted that many of his co-workers were also servants: the woman Phoebe, although when the KJV reads the word *diakonos* linked to a woman, it is for some strange reason translated helper (see Romans 16:1).

Other men like Tychicus, (Ephesians 6:21, Colossians 4:7) Timothy, (1 Timothy 4:6) and Epaphras, were called *diakonos*, just like Phoebe

(Colossians 1:7). Jesus said that all of his followers should be *diakonos* (Matthew 20:26, 23:11 and John 12:26), which means that a servant's spirit should characterize all of us. So, with all Christians doing the work of a deacon (*diakonos*) as deacons of Christ, deacons of His message, and deacons of one another, one is hard-pressed to find authority over in that word.

You can see there is no hint in the New Testament of anyone holding an office called deacon which gives one authority over other Christians. Since that is the case, where did the idea of the office of deacon come from in our churches?

FRAUDULENT AUTHORITY

There are a couple of places where the King James Version translates the word *diakonos* in a manner that goes well beyond the true meaning of the word and winds up adding concepts to the original text that were never intended. One place is in 1 Timothy 3:13 where Paul says:

"For they that *have used the office of a deacon* well purchase to themselves a good degree, and great boldness in the faith which is in Christ Jesus" (I Timothy 3:13).

The seven words, "have used the office of a deacon" were all used to translate (and define) one Greek word, *diakoneo*, which according to the Greek scholar A. H. Strong is a word which means: "To be a servant, attendant, domestic, to serve, wait upon."

W.E. Vine adds this about the word *diakonia*, "The Revised Version rightly omits office and translates the verb *diakoneo* to mean simply to serve." Notice, the Greek scholar W.E. Vine admits that the word "office" is not found in verse.

Throughout the entire New Testament, the word *diakoneo* is NEVER used to imply or show an office, and it certainly doesn't imply rule. It is the service done by one who is a servant to another person.

The phrase translated *"they that have used the office of a deacon"* (I Timothy 3:13) seems to be an attempt by the King James Version translators to identify an office of the Anglican Church that was already in operation at the time of translation, and to continue it by including a phrase in the text to support it.

Thus, hierarchical offices of authority in the church *are assumed* by the King James Version translators, but such

FRAUDULENT AUTHORITY

offices of authority in the church *are not unauthorized* by the writers of the New Testament.

I will restate the problem with the word "office" in the English versions of the New Testament.

Because having an office of authority in the church called deacons was the cultural bias and desire of King James and the scholars he enlisted to translate the Bible, the translator's hierarchical view of authority in the church made its way into the King James Version.

Their concept of church authority is nowhere to be found in the sacred Scriptures, but this system of authority had already become a hierarchical religious system by 1611. The translators practiced what is called eisegesis in their translation of the Greek into English, which means they read something into the text that is not there.

Likewise, in the King James Version of 1 Timothy 3:1, Paul is wrongly recorded saying, *"This is a true saying, If a man desires the office of a bishop, he desires a good work."*

Again, the word "office is "not present in I Timothy 3:1.

The Greek word translated bishop is the single word *episkopos*, which means "to tend or to oversee." So the word office was incorrectly placed in the verse, and the word bishop was used to translate oversee, because the translators had bishops in King James' day, and it seems that King James and his men wished to maintain their hierarchical positions of authority in the church.

FRAUDULENT AUTHORITY

A proper translation of 1 Timothy 3:1 would simply be, *"If a person sets their heart on overseeing, it is an honorable work they desire to do."*

There is no office of bishop at all in the text. It is just a person desiring a ministry of overseeing to which the Apostle is referring.

The only other instance in the New Testament where the the English word "office" occurs is in Romans 12:4 where the KJV says, *"For as we have many members in one body, and all members have not the same office."*

But the English word office in this verse DOES NOT properly translate the Greek word at all. The Greek word being translated "office" in Romans 12:14 is the word "praxis," which means "a doing or deed or function."

It is the same word used in Romans 8:13, "...for if you live according to the flesh you will die, but if by the Spirit you put to death *the deeds* (praxis) of the body, you will live."

Simply put, the office of pastor/elder/bishop or deacon, as an office that conveys inherent authority in the church, simply does not exist in the Bible.

FRAUDULENT AUTHORITY

Chapter 7: Nobody Rules Over Anyone Else in the Body of Christ (Hebrews 13)

The biggest proof-text for the idea of someone ruling, (being over others in authority) in the church and particularly with the elders doing so, is found in Hebrews 13:7, 17, 24. These verses say:

> "Remember them which have the *rule over you*, who have spoken unto you the word of God: whose faith follow, considering the end of their conversation."
> (Hebrews 13:7)

> "Obey them that have the *rule over you*, and submit yourselves: for they watch for your souls, as they that must give account, that they may do it with joy, and not with grief: for that is unprofitable for you."
> (Hebrews 13:17)

> "Salute (to draw to one's self) all them that have the *rule over you*, and all the saints. They of Italy salute you." (Hebrews 13:24)

There are several observations to make about the above three verses:

1). The word elder or pastor does not appear in these verses. Not once. It simply is not there. To justify where a pastor or elder can rule over anybody, one needs to point out where a pastor or elder is mentioned in this text, and it can't be done.

2). The word *"over"* is not actually in any one of these three verses, so we must lay it aside as an unfortunate and an unwarranted addition to the text by translators because the Greek word for "over" is simply not there in the original text.

3). It's also worthy of note that Hebrews 13:7 verse is written in the *past tense* though incorrectly translated by the KJV in the present tense. The verse is correctly translated this way:

> "Remember those *who were* your guides (past tense), *whose* faith you are to imitate, taking note of how they were faithful to the very end of life" (Hebrews 13:7).

Hebrews 13:7 is a verse that is reminding the Hebrew Christians of all those mentioned in chapters 11 and 12, and it follows verse 6 which refers to not fearing man, which these people did not do, and gave their lives because of being fearless. It may even include the Apostles themselves.

But to make guides to mean "elders" or "pastors" is an addition to the text, and in the rules of proper biblical interpretation, pastors or elders is not an option since they are not mentioned either in the text or in the context.

4). In Hebrews 13:17 three words give some trouble as translated in the King James Version. As mentioned above, the word "over" is not in the text - so we will drop it. The three English words that were chosen to be used by King James translators are: Obey, rule and submit.

Obey

"Obey" translates the Greek word *peitho*. This word means "to persuade, to win over." When it is in the passive and middle voices, it means to be persuaded, to listen to (in Acts 5:40 *peitho* is in the passive voice and is translated "they agreed").

The obedience suggested in the text (Hebrews 13:17) is not a submission to any authority, but an agreement resulting from persuasion (see W. E. Vine's Expository Dictionary of New Testament Words).

So, according to Vine's Dictionary, it means to follow because of being persuaded. It does not mean obedience the way the western mind thinks of obedience. The obedience of Hebrews 13:17 is due to internal reasoning and agreement that results from persuasion, not external conformity that results from authoritative control.

Rule

"Rule" translates the Greek word *hegeomai*. This word means "to lead, to go before, to be a leader." This word does not carry the connotation of ruling over, but that of giving leadership in a church (see Strong's Word Studies). So, according to Strong again, true leadership is nothing more than going on ahead.

Submit

"Submit" translates the Greek word *hypeikete*. This word is in the present imperative active tense, and it means "to choose to submit or to follow or to yield." Hebrews 13:17 is the only place where the Greek word *hypeikete* makes an appearance in the New Testament, and most likely should be translated *"yield."*

There is a Greek word that means to be subject to and obey. It is *peitharcheo* (pith-ar-KAY-o), one of the words built upon *arche,* which means ruler. It is found three times in the New

Testament, twice in Acts (5:29 & 27:21) and once in Titus (3:1).

In these places as well as other writings outside the New Testament, it describes obedience to someone who is in civil authority or to God, but that word is not the word used here in Hebrews.

Even Paul counted himself as a fellow servant. He said in II Corinthians 1:24, "Not that we have dominion [*archo*] over your faith, but are fellow workers for your joy, for by faith you stand."

5). For a better understanding of Hebrews 13:24 see the above for Hebrews 13:7 and the meaning of the Greek word translated rule.

So the better translation of the Greek language in these verses would be:

> *"Remember those who were* (past tense) *your guides, who led the way with the Word: whose faith imitate, considering the strong way they ended their life."*
> (Hebrews 13:7)

> *"Choose to yield to those who are out in front leading you because you are persuaded they are likewise being faithful in their task, knowing they will be held accountable."* (Hebrews 13:17)

> *"Embrace all those who are your guides or leaders, as well as all the Saints. They of Italy embrace you as well."*
> (Hebrews 13:24)

FRAUDULENT AUTHORITY

There is no concept of lording authority over someone in the church.

There is simply NO TEXTUAL justification for an office of any kind in the New Testament local church with an *inherent authority* vested in it.

This is not to say there are not ministries that can be called pastoral or elder ministries or even deacon ministries in a local church.

What can be said is that any New Testament local church "authority" is something different than our cultural concept of authority, which is someone being "over" someone else.

Christ alone is over His people, individually and corporately. Only when pastors and religious leaders understand the harmful damage Fraudulent Authority brings to followers of Jesus will the church of Jesus Christ regain her transformative power.

Chapter 8: Real Authority in the Church

The scriptural model for church life is one where grace-gifted people, anointed by the Spirit and recognized by the people, function as gifted leaders in the body of Christ, teaching and equipping ALL in the body to do the work of ministry as described in Ephesians 4:11- 13:

"So Christ himself gave the apostles, the prophets, the evangelists, the pastors and teachers, *to equip His people for works of service*, so that the body of Christ may be built up until we all reach unity in the faith and in the knowledge of the Son of God and become mature, attaining to the whole measure of the fullness of Christ" (Ephesians 4:11-13).

This kind of church ministry far different than a few officeholders doing the work of ministry and all the people doing what they are told by those in office. The biblical model of the church moves one from viewing the church as an organization or institution to seeing her as an organism or a body, properly called the Body of Christ.

Authority is to be experienced in the assembly *because of the gifts and ministries of the Holy Spirit becoming obvious through people as they serve the whole of the body*.

In one sense, the entire body shares authority (Ephesians 5:21, 1 Peter 5:5). This means we recognize one another's gifts, knowledge, or experience in the Lord and we choose to serve/ submit because the Holy Spirit has placed some people as gifted leaders among us, anointing their humble service to others.

That is the key to understanding Bishops/ Pastors/Elders/ Deacons and their function. No one has spiritual authority over anybody BECAUSE they hold an office. Authority certainly doesn't come because someone has a stronger personality, knows more Bible, or is held in high esteem. That is foreign to the New Testament.

Paul, the Apostle himself, had to defend his Apostleship by his work being the result of the Spirit gifting him for such service. 1 Timothy 5:17 speaks of those elders "that give oversight well... are worthy of double honor."

It is because they "give oversight well" they have authority in the congregation. This oversight is a result of the Holy Spirit's anointing, and the people see the Spirit's giftings in the leader through gifts, the humility of character, and gentle persuasion.

In other words, the anointing of the Spirit makes clear the authority that rests on a ministry done well, not an office that is held by someone.

What about Elders in the Congregation?

Someone may ask, "But doesn't Acts 20:28 indicate that the elders were over the congregation?"

In that verse, we are told, *"Take heed therefore unto yourselves, and to all the flock, over* **[en]** *which the Holy Spirit has made you overseers, to feed the church of God, which he hath purchased with His own blood"* (Acts 20:28).

This little Greek word **"en"** translated *"over"* in Acts 20:28 is used 2,700 times in the New Testament and is nowhere else translated "over." It is a simple Greek preposition which means *in or among*.

Peter instructed the elders to be very careful that elders don't "lord it over" the flock (see 1 Peter 5:3).

So what we have in the text is an authority that is to be experienced in the assembly because the gifts and ministries of the Holy Spirit that are made obvious through people.

As said before, in one sense, the entire body shares authority (Ephesians 5:21, 1 Peter 5:5).

This means we recognize one another's gifts, knowledge, or experience in the Lord, and we choose to serve/submit to one another because the Holy Spirit has placed us all as gifts to the body in some fashion and anointed our ministries and gifts.

What a tragedy that we have accepted a hierarchy of rulers in the local Church, which ends up limiting the freedom of so many members of the Church.

Then, to add insult to injury, the ruled ones have their spirituality measured by their submission to the authority of those rulers instead of measuring the authority of leaders by their submission to the Lord.

This is primarily because the present-day view of the church is one where the church is seen as being an **institution or organization run by leaders** who are of a corporate chief executive officer's mentality that is, as has been shown, completely foreign to the scriptures.

Only Christ has authority.

FRAUDULENT AUTHORITY

Principles to Remember

1). There is only one Head of the Church, and all authority has been given to Him. If anyone ever assumes authority because of their person or position they are usurping the authority of the Head (Ephesians 4:5, 15).

2). The Head of the Body has given an authoritative Word to the members of the Body (universal or local). The Old and New Testaments are the inspired Word of God, and followers of Jesus are bound to the words of Jesus Christ. As the Father said, "Hear ye Him," and what Jesus says is in the New Covenant writings (Hebrews 1:2, Acts 18:28).

3). All believers are responsible to the Head of the Church [Christ] individually and have a responsibility to each other called the "one anothers" of the New Testament (Romans 14:4, Ephesians 5:21).

4). All believers are priests and are gifted. Therefore, all must take their place among the body members to minister for the good of one another (1 Corinthians 12-14).

5). There are certain ones (without regard to gender) who are gifted to serve and guide the body of Christ in unique ways. Whether they are pastor/elder/bishop/deacon, the purpose of these persons and their gifts are to serve the whole body by equipping all saints for the work of ministry (Ephesians 4:11-12).

6). There is no emphasis in the New Testament on spiritual authority derived from any office or position in the church. The King James Version uses the word office, but it is not in the text at all, and it would be better NOT to use it at all.

FRAUDULENT AUTHORITY

7). The state will recognize licensed ministers whom the church has set apart for this purpose, but all members are ministers of Christ.

The rule in church life should be the Headship of Christ, the priesthood of all believers, with each member contributing his or her giftedness and edifying each other, under the Spirit's anointing, giving no regard to office, race, or gender.

It is legitimate to set up any system that a local fellowship desires to carry out the state's business. However, real church ministry occurs under the anointing of the Spirit as we serve one another through body life, and then move into the community to share the gospel of Jesus Christ.

Understanding where authority resides and from where it comes must not be simply a theory, but it must become a practice if we are to reflect the reality of Christ to a lost world in need of the gospel.

Check any leadership by this standard if you want to be biblical in church life.

Chapter 9: It Takes a Village Covenant to Raise a Bitter Root

Every church's worst nightmare is to hear of a fellow church member who falls into immoral sexual activity. Village Church in Dallas, Texas recently experienced such a nightmare. What happened when Village Church attempted to deal with the problem of a church missionary involved in child pornography vividly illustrates the problems that occur when pastors or elders wrongly believe they have "authority over" people in their church.

Jordan Root and his wife Karen Root were missionaries from Village Church, working with SIM (Serving in Mission) in East Asia. Jordan Root confessed to the extensive viewing of child pornography, a crime in the United States and most nations of the world. Jordan was terminated by SIM and sent back to the United States. Jordan Root denies he ever sexually molested any young girls, but his extensive ministry and personal involvement with pre-puberty teens caused his wife concern that he had not fully confessed the depths of his involvement in either child sexual abuse or child pornography.

It seems Village Church pastors and elders attempted--in the beginning--to perform their diligence in giving pastoral care to both Jordan and Karen. However, unless you've been the partner in a marriage where your spouse has been involved in child pornography for years, it's difficult to understand the pain, fear, and distrust present in the heart and mind of Karen Root.

FRAUDULENT AUTHORITY

After returning to the United States, Karen Root filed for an annulment of her marriage to Jordan Root. In the State of Texas, if it is proven that a spouse deceived a partner before marriage, an annulment can be granted. An annulment is a state's declaration that a covenant of marriage never took place (void) due to deception.

The State of Texas approved the annulment, and Karen Root changed her name back to Karen Hinkley. Karen then resigned her membership from Village Church, preferring to attend church at a place other than where Jordan attended. I'm glad the state of Texas granted the annulment, but in my opinion, even if they had not, Karen had grounds for divorce.

Here's where it gets weird.

Village Church elders sent a letter to Karen Hinkley. In that letter, they informed Karen of three things:

(1). The church officers were perplexed as to why Karen "filed for an annulment."

(2). Karen was "now under discipline" for violating the "church covenant."

(3). The church officers, therefore "cannot accept Karen's resignation" from church membership.

I normally do not write about issues involving other churches. However, I have broken my normal pattern over this problem within Village Church to throw a lifeline to pastors of other churches who face similar situations.

Karen Hinkley seemed to be reasonable, smart, and I would even say 'classy' in her Christian faith. You could sense this in her letters to her pastors and elders, all of which were public in an online forum. I later would discover that Karen was exactly like I pictured her to be through reading her letters.

Village Church pastors/elders made some huge mistakes because they thought they were supposed to "rule over" people like Karen. The Bible doesn't grant pastors any spiritual authority over anyone, but if you wrongly believe you have it, you'll make some stupid mistakes.

Village elders made the mistake of believing Karen couldn't divorce her husband *without their permission.*

But even worse for Village, they were in dangerous territory legally by not allowing Karen to withdraw from membership because she was under discipline for not seeking out counsel from the elders who "rule over" her.

The 1989 *Guinn v. Church of Christ Collinsville* is a legal case where a woman 'resigned her membership' from her home church. It has similarities and a few dissimilarities with Village Church versus Hinkley, which is not yet--and hopefully won't be- -a legal case. The Church of Christ in Collinsville (Oklahoma) told an adulterous woman in their church that they "could not accept her resignation because she was under church discipline."

The adulterous woman then sued her church. In the end, the woman was awarded a settlement in the hundreds of thousands of dollars because the church refused to accept her resignation. Though the verdict was overturned in the appellate court, the appellate judges based their decision to overturn on the fact the adulterous woman was already under church discipline.

FRAUDULENT AUTHORITY

This is where the Village Church pastors and elders got themselves into legal trouble. They'd gone after the victim, not the offender. Karen Hinckley was not "in sin."

Of course, the elders and pastors of Village argued that Karen was in sin and needed church "discipline" because she filed for "an annulment" for her marriage without seeking permission from the spiritual authority over her (e.g. "pastors and elders").

The State of Texas had already sided with Karen on the annulment. Her refusal to seek pastoral counsel in terms of restoring her relationship with Jordan, a confessed child pornographer, was a big issue for Village elders and pastors.

However, it led the pastors and elders to make an even bigger mistake. A big, BIG, mistake. The State of Texas had already sided with Karen in terms of the annulment. The State of Texas would not smile on Village *for sending out a letter to 6,000 members accusing Karen of wrongdoing*, even though they might claim their discipline of Karen was an ecclesiastical (church) matter.

At the time this all happened, I offered some unsolicited advice to the elders and pastors of Village. I suggested they take my advice to protect them litigation that every attorney with a shingle on his window would love to take against them.

It seemed to me that Karen didn't want to harm Village Church or anyone else. She just wanted people to take child sexual abuse seriously.

Here was my advice to Village elders and pastors:

FRAUDULENT AUTHORITY

(1). Write an immediate letter of apology--and I meant immediate-- to Karen Hinckley, retracting the earlier letter, and informing Karen that they are indeed accepting Karen's resignation from their church.

(2). Never speak on behalf of Karen Hinckley again--to anyone- -including the members of their congregation.

(3). Realize that your 501c-3 called Village Church is not equivalent to the Kingdom of God. Yes, Village Church plays a huge and vital role in His Kingdom, but their non-profit and His Kingdom are not synonymous. Therefore, next time anyone decides they wish to leave their non-profit, let them go.

As a side note, I encouraged Village pastors to continue their ministry to Jordan Root. Unlike some, I believed the pastors had an interest in the victims of his abuse. Some of my friends had a hard time believing that Village leaders were concerned for the victims because they'd taken one of Jordan's victims -- his wife - - to the proverbial gates of hell because she dared disagree with how they were progressing in their ministry toward her and her former husband.

I encouraged the Village elders and Pastor Matt Chandler to admit their wrong views on "spiritual authority" and apologize to Karen Hinckley. I suggested they accept her resignation of membership. I then encouraged them to stop viewing their office as pastor/elder of Village Church as the ultimate authority in the Kingdom of God.

Jesus Christ was Karen Hinckley's ultimate authority, and He had led her to resign her membership.

"Don't argue with Jesus," I said.

FRAUDULENT AUTHORITY

Village Church eventually did the very thing I encouraged them to do. Whether they ever read what I wrote about the situation at the time, I don't know. But I do believe many church pastors and leaders could save themselves a great deal of heartache by refusing to see themselves as "ruling over" anyone in their churches.

Chapter 10: Five Reasons to Say "No" to a Church Covenant

"But I tell you, do not swear an oath at all ... All you need to say is simply 'Yes' or 'No'; anything beyond this comes from the evil one." These are Jesus words in Matthew 5:34-37.

Village Church in Dallas, Texas placed a member named Karen Root under church discipline because she annulled her marriage with a confessed child pornographer. A letter Village Church elders sent to members gave their logic for placing Karen under church discipline.

The elders believed they had no choice because Karen **violated the church covenant** that she signed when she joined Village Church. Specifically, Karen violated the covenant by not getting church leaders' permission to file for an annulment. The elders wrote:

"...Karen filed for an immediate annulment of her marriage to Jordan apart from the counsel of the church... (by) signing the Membership Covenant, a member agrees ... to receive our care..."

Karen had respectfully requested withdrawal of membership from Village Church, but the elders wouldn't allow it because she had not sought their counsel. She refused to come "under their care," so they put Karen under discipline. No Village Church member under discipline, wrote Village church authorities, can "withdraw" from membership. Therefore, Village pastors/elders "refused to accept" Karen's request to withdraw from Village membership.

FRAUDULENT AUTHORITY

This was an ugly situation all the way around. Village Church leaders--regardless of the vocal criticism they receive--believed they were men of integrity. They were, in their minds, fulfilling their pastoral role and abiding by the church covenant they had demanded everyone sign before they became members. Some who are not members of Village blamed Karen for signing a church covenant. Nobody should blame Karen. She, like other evangelicals, probably had no idea of the ultimate consequences of signing church covenants.

The guilt for this fiasco at Village lies with church authorities who demand signatures from prospective members that turned their spiritual formation and maturation over to mere men instead of the Holy Spirit.

I read Village's Church Covenant. It's chilling when it comes to the authority of elders and church leaders.

Here are some of the phrases that the prospective member must read and then sign, vowing their allegiance to obey:

- I understand the importance of submission to church leadership
- I will submit to the elders and other appointed leaders of the church
- I will agree to walk through the steps of marriage reconciliation at The Village Church before pursuing a divorce from my spouse

The premise of this book is that the major problem in modern evangelical Christianity is the authoritarianism of evangelical leaders. I have sought to explain how pastors or elders "twist the Scriptures" and demand "obedience and

FRAUDULENT AUTHORITY

submission" to this alleged authority. Jesus tells us that that true 'spiritual leaders' are only servants, never masters.

Evangelical leaders seem not to be listening to Jesus.

I want to give you five reasons why I would never sign a church membership covenant to become a member.

(1). A church covenant makes the Holy Spirit irrelevant in my life.

We are called in Scripture to be led "by the Spirit." Though "there is wisdom in the counsel of many," when I sign a church covenant I abdicate my right to hear from the Spirit myself. When Karen Root resigned her membership from Village, she stated: "I have sought the Lord diligently and several godly people I trust."

That wasn't good enough for Village elders; Karen didn't seek them out. A church covenant fetters one's ability to seek the Spirit's wisdom and advice from godly people other than the elders and pastors of the church that demanded you to sign.

(2). A church covenant replaces my one true Mediator with inferior mediators.

I have only One High Priest who stands between God and me - Jesus, the Son of God - and anyone who comes between Jesus and me as I walk by His counsel and His wisdom is a detriment to my growth. A true servant in the Kingdom will only and always point me to Jesus Christ for my marching orders, and will never demand that I accept their orders as from God. When I sign a church covenant, I'm in essence handing over the authority of Jesus Christ in my life to mere men.

(3). A church covenant makes the institutional church equivalent to the Kingdom of God.

A 501c-3 non-profit institutional church plays an important role in the Kingdom of God, but the local church is not the kingdom of God. Anyone who knows history understands that institutional churches who demand spiritual authority over individual believers have wrongly placed their institution on par with God's Kingdom.

For example, the great 17th-century Baptist hymn writer and theologian Benjamin Keach decided to write a book for children containing evangelical truth. Authorities of the Church of England sought to execute him for writing that infant baptism was not biblical.

On what basis could the Church of England kill Benjamin Keach?

Answer: The same basis Village Church can consign Karen Root to church discipline. Leaders of the 17th century Church of England and the 21st century Village Church both believe their institution is equivalent to the Kingdom of God. Their leaders falsely believe that they hold the keys of life and death and of heaven and hell. It isn't so.

Don't sign a covenant and perpetuate this dangerous lie.

(4). A church covenant by its nature is designed to protect an authoritarian structure.

When a Christian agrees to a church covenant that demands submission to elders/pastors, he or she is enabling that institutional church to maintain an authoritarian structure.

FRAUDULENT AUTHORITY

Rather than the weak and wounded sheep being the focus of attention within the church, most modern covenants are written with phrases that seem intent on bringing church members into "submission to church authorities."

Quickly scan any church covenant. If "submission to church elders" is anywhere found, then know the covenant is designed to keep control of members and maintain the authority of the leaders. Paul Burleson points out that any institutional church more concerned with supporting their authoritarian system of control than healing their wounded members is sending signals of weak spiritual leadership.

Jesus said that the world uses titles, positions of honor, and seeks to "exercise authority over those they rule," but "this should never be the case among His followers (Mark 10:35-45).

(5). A church covenant requires something more than a simple "Yes" or "No."

Jesus said that anything you have to do that goes beyond your simple words of "Yes" and "No" is from the "evil one" (Matthew 5:37). When I join a church, I will forever refuse to sign any document, whether it be a "tithing card," or "a membership covenant," or any other document that requires a vow from me regarding my future performance or activity.

If I ever attend a church that requires such a thing, I will refuse to join by a principle I follow. I will live freely, speak with integrity, and rest in the simplicity of following Jesus and living by the Spirit. Written vows will not fetter me to a church that is seeking to protect their authority over me.

FRAUDULENT AUTHORITY

I need no covenant to guarantee that God will finish the work He's begun in me.

Chapter 11: Authority in the New Testament

I gained an Internet friend through my online writings regarding "church authority." Fob James is the son of a two-term Alabama Governor. He is a follower of Jesus and one very smart attorney. He wrote various "pro bono" briefs for his governor father during the seventies and then again during the nineties, concentrating on church-state cases.

Fob pointed out to me that attorneys change legal vernacular all the time to promote personal agendas and he believes theologians are no more prone, to be honest with scriptural language than lawyers are with legal language.

Fob forwarded to me an article he wrote on church authority, permitting me to publish it for my readers. Fob and his wife have discovered several interesting things about so-called "spiritual authority" in churches over the last few years.

Fob believes the unbiblical and worldly concept of authority has its roots in the human desire to "dominate and control" and control others. Fob believes Christian living, both inside and outside the institutional church, should be opposite of the kinds of authority which the world understands.

We don't dominate or control; we serve. Fob's writings give further reasons to avoid signing church covenants or make promises that you will "submit" to those in authority.

Read on…

FRAUDULENT AUTHORITY

In the New Covenant scriptures, only the apostle Paul speaks of "authority" (*exousia*) in the context of leadership in the churches.

The most descriptive words he uses to describe that "authority," which he (and others) exercise with tenderness and tears and sometimes toughness, are the words "authority in the gospel" (1 Cor. 9:18) and "authority is given... [by the Lord]...for edification and not destruction." (2 Cor. 10:8, 13:10).

The words "authority in the church" or their equivalent cannot be found in scripture.

In fact, "church" (*ekklesia*) and "authority" (*exousia*) never even appear in juxtaposition in the scriptures.

The word "authority" (*exousia*) is never mentioned regarding elders, pastors, deacons, prophets, local churches, or even any apostles, except for Paul himself and those who labored with him in the gospel.

Not even Peter is said to have had "authority," even though Peter clearly had authority in the gospel in fact. "Keys" and "Open Doors" for instance signify authority.

The word "authority" (*exousia*) is mentioned in the Revelation of John, when "overcomers" in the church of Thyatira will be given "authority over the nations," at the judgment of the world, to rule them with a "rod of iron" (Revelation 2:26).

FRAUDULENT AUTHORITY

Evidently, a lot of people for a long time have wanted to get a head start on their potential reward at the end of days and rule not the world, but the church, with a" rod of iron" until the end comes.

The common lingo of today (and almost the last 2000 years) such as "church authority" or "church government" would sound weird to the writers of the New Testament.

I think this lingo also grieves the Holy Spirit because it isn't His words. It is clear that the Holy Spirit backs up those who have authority "in the gospel."

No church membership covenant or the like can substitute for the real authority that comes from the Holy Spirit. Many who actually do the work of the Lord today do not have titles. But they do have authority in the gospel.

And by the way, we all have been given a gospel commission - it can be found in Matthew 28. Another especially meaningful assignment for all of us is found in 1 Corinthians 15:58. It reads, "Therefore, my beloved brethren, be steadfast, immovable, always abounding in the work of the Lord, knowing that your labor is not in vain in the Lord."

The biggest eye-opener to me on "authority" came when I was noticing Paul's constant language about things "in the Lord."

"In the Lord?" What is the significance of this phrase?

I went to a bible website called "Blue Letter Bible" and read every occurrence of the words "In the Lord" (or equivalents such as In Him, In Christ, In Whom, In God, In Jesus, etc.) in scripture. There are over 250 instances of these terms.

FRAUDULENT AUTHORITY

In contrast, there are about a dozen instances of "in the church."

I do not detract from the importance of "in the church," but point out that "in the church" has been extensively used by American "theologians" (of almost every evangelical stripe) to the exclusion of the words actually chosen by the Holy Spirit for a lot of things believers should do.

For instance, do the scriptures talk about "receiving one another," that is, other believers, "in the church" or "in the Lord?"

Look it up.

Go further and read all 250+ occurrences of "in the Lord" and its equivalents (In Him, In Christ, In Whom, In God, In Jesus), and see what it does in your heart. See what it does to your fear of man. See what it does for your understanding of "authority" and every group out there that requires you to promise to submit to their "authority" as a condition for being allowed into the "group."

The scriptures teach mutual submission among believers, and proper respect, indeed esteem, for true leadership/eldership as exemplified by Paul and the other writers of the scriptures. The scriptures do not teach a "covenant of submission" to anyone.

You submit as warranted by scripture; you do not make a vow or covenant to submit to a man.

There is a lot more to say about this. Suffice it for now: the Galatian error remains with us. Supplemental covenants to recognize "church authority" or "make a radical commitment

FRAUDULENT AUTHORITY

to the local church," etc., are everywhere in America, among just about every group.

These supplemental covenants are the true "foundations" of many turf-driven works of the flesh.

The end result is that they substitute a work of the flesh for that of the Spirit.

The ecclesiological "commitment" (*paratithemi*) that scripture actually teaches is a commitment to the scriptures themselves, which is a commitment to the gospel.

The gospel is that Jesus died for our sins according to the scriptures, that He was buried, and that He rose from the dead on the third day according to the scriptures, inaugurating for all a new Way of living. It is the New Covenant way of life, sealed in His body and blood alone that the Holy Spirit honors.

This is the Covenant the Lord told us to remember and proclaim until He comes again.

So, next time someone says that you need an extra authority-covenant, or extra unity-commitment, or the like, to be fully admitted to "their" fellowship, don't fall for it.

If they press you, you might also consider telling them this — "IT IS FINISHED."

———

Chapter 12: Who Is the Boss at Your Church?

When one is asked "Who governs your church?" the typical response is "Jesus Christ." Granted, Jesus is the Lord of all believers, but next time you're at a church business meeting, try pointing your finger at Jesus and then tell your fellow church members that He needs to take over.

They'd look at you like you were Charlie Sheen.

Ideally, Jesus Christ controls the hearts, minds, and tongues of all those conducting church business. But the question remains:

"Who is it that governs your church?"

The subject of church polity is complex. Some churches have bishops who take their orders from higher authorities in the synod.

Other churches have what they call 'ruling' elders. A few churches have one person that rules the church like King Xerxes ruled Persia. However, the biblical model for church governance is congregational. Many neo-reformed evangelicals have moved to 'ruling elders,' setting a group of men aside as the "spiritual and moral authority" for the church.

In my opinion, this is a huge mistake.

The scripture teaches every member of the church has equal moral and spiritual authority. The church is a democracy of

FRAUDULENT AUTHORITY

equals, not an oligarchy of superiors. Congregationalism alone represents this sense of equality.
The word congregation means "the act of assembling."

One can easily interchange the words assembly and congregation. For example, an assembly of God is a congregation of God, and both phrases refer to what we now call a church. Here is where it gets interesting. In the Bible, the English word church translates the Greek word ekklesia.

What does the word *ekklesia* mean?

Surprise! It means an assembly or congregation of people with equal authority.

Let me state this important principle again: By the very definition of the word church (*ekklesia*), a church is a congregation or assembly of people with equal authority. Let me prove it.

In 510 B.C. the city-state of Athens was ruled by a tyrant named Hippias. The people of Athens revolted, and with the help of soldiers from Sparta, Athenians expelled the dictator Hippias from the city. Cleisthenes, who followed Hippias as chief ruler of Athens, instituted amazing reforms in the city and he became known as "The Father of Democracy." Cleisthenes established the Assembly (Ekklesia) of Athens.

This ekklesia became the meeting place where ordinary citizens could speak their minds and try to influence one another in the affairs of Athens.

The Ekklesia assembled at the *Pnyx*, an open-air theatre with a retaining wall and orator's stand west of the Acropolis of Athens. Every member of the Assembly could speak, but those who were over fifty years in age were allowed to go first in honor of their wisdom and maturity.

Elders in the Assembly did not mean those with more authority; it meant those with greater wisdom.

The Assembly believed no one person should have more authority or power. If an individual gained too much power in the Ekklesia, he would be voted out and exiled from Athens for ten years. In a world filled with despots and tyrants, Athenian congregationalism was the marvel of the world!

It is no accident that when the biblical writers chose a word to represent believers of Jesus Christ who congregate or assemble, they chose the word *ekklesia*. This word did not just drop from heaven.

It was not used by Paul or Peter or James in a vacuum. They knew the word represented an assembly of people who shared in equal authority and equal privileges within the Kingdom. Paul even went further than the Athenian Assembly in his teaching that the assembly of Christ (the church) should be a place where there is no difference between Jews and Greeks, males or females, slave or free (Galatians 3:28).

It is completely contrary to Scripture to believe that some men have been given more moral and spiritual authority than other believers within the church. In the ekklesia of Jesus Christ, any person, male or female, recognized as being in Christ carries as much moral and spiritual authority as any other person--no more, no less--the same.

FRAUDULENT AUTHORITY

The state may recognize trustees with greater legal authority, or pastors with greater state authority (the officiant in marriages, etc.) or signatures bearing corporate authority (deeds, title, etc.), but God established in his *ekklesia* a group of people with equal spiritual authority.

Pay attention to those who are older and wiser in the ekklesia of Christ.

Minister to those around you with a servant's heart and attitude. But if you ever begin to feel that somebody is beginning to exert spiritual authority and power over you and other individuals in an attempt to govern Christ's church, then it is time to confront the abuser of the ekklesia and call him out, and maybe even put him out.

My friend wrote a bestselling book called *The Subtle Power of Spiritual Abuse*, but maybe another one needs to be written entitled The Subtle Problem of Not Confronting Spiritual Abuse. A healthy *ekklesia* won't allow any abuse of power. It's not easy confronting abusers, but for the good of the *ekklesia,* it must be done.

Chapter 13: Ordination, the Mother of Fraudulent Authority

The unbiblical thinking in some quarters regarding church "authority," "ordination," and "women in ministry" is profound and dangerous in terms of the advancement of God's Kingdom.

Rather than acknowledging that authority flows from Christ, and that the power to transform lives for the Kingdom comes from Christ as His people minister and serve as the Spirit gifts us, many evangelical churches are looking more and more like institutions of authoritarian control and domination of others rather than a symmetrical body with healthy functions that bring life to others.

In Roman Catholic teaching, the church possesses spiritual authority on earth, the Pope decrees authoritative bulls, and a hierarchy of authority flows down from the Pope to the parish priests who are the sole authority on spiritual matters in the parish.

Roman Catholic teaching on spiritual authority is absolutely contrary to the Bible.

What's amazing is the number of evangelicals who claim to hold to *Sola Scriptura,* yet they claim to have spiritual authority over people like the Pope claims to have spiritual authority over the Roman Catholic Church.

According to Scripture, there is only One head of the Church or local churches and all authority is His, given to Him by God the Father.

FRAUDULENT AUTHORITY

For a man or woman in the church to possess any kind of "authority," it must come from Christ because He has "all authority." Christ's *authority is not dispensed by the church's bestowal of any office*, but by the Spirit who dispenses spiritual gifts that empower *believers to serve others* in the power of Christ.

In short, the authority of Christ in the world is always evidenced by service, for Jesus said, *"The greatest among you shall be your servant"* (Matthew 23:11).

When the church recognizes the gifts of the Spirit in a person that enables and compels them to serve the body of Christ or the world in general, then the church sets that person aside for particular service by the laying on of hands.

This setting aside for service or ministry within the church (teaching, shepherding, serving), or sometimes in the world (evangelizing, missions, etc.) is simply the Body's recognition that Christ's power has already been bestowed through the dispensing of unique spiritual gifts.

Unfortunately, many in the evangelical church have succumbed to the error of the Roman Catholic Church by calling this setting aside of God's servants to ministry with the word 'ordination' and assume that 'ordination' bestows some magical power or an alleged spiritual authority.

This so-called power, according to those who hold to this belief, is always assigned to an 'office' that has been reached via the ordination. Accordingly, only those set aside by the church to this office have the authority they need to minister or serve others.

So, according to this very unbiblical and narrow ecclesiological thinking, only ordained pastors have the authority to do pastoral ministry.
The problem of those who push for the prohibition of women pastoring other people is the belief that the only people who have the "authority" to pastor are those who have been given that "office" of authority by the church.

Because of this unbiblical view of authority and an office of authority within the church, many conservative Bible-believing Christians wrongly believe:

1). No missionary has the 'authority' to baptize but those who occupy the "office" of pastor or elder.

2). No believer has the 'authority' to dispense the Lord's Supper but those who occupy the "office" of pastor or elder.

3). No student of Scripture, particularly female, has the 'authority' to teach the Bible, but those who occupy the "office" of pastor or elder.

4). No chaplain has the 'authority' to minister to people but those who occupy the "office" of pastor or elder.

Nowhere in Scripture is this idea of a mystical 'office' of spiritual authority taught.

Let me repeat.

Nowhere in the inspired, infallible, sufficient Word of God is the idea taught that the power or authority to minister or serve is associated with an office that is received through ordination.

FRAUDULENT AUTHORITY

The ordinances (commands) to baptize and remember Him through the Lord's Supper are Christ's commands to all His followers, not the church's commands to "ordained" people.

The church's responsibility is to acknowledge and appreciate all the gifted people in the body of Christ, regardless of gender.

The Kingdom of Christ advances under the Lordship of Christ, not the oversight of institutional authorities.

"I will build my church," Jesus said, but in modern evangelicalism, it seems that Jesus is replaced by "ordained" men in an "office of authority" who see the church as an institution over which they rule.

The further you move toward New Testament Christianity, the further away you move from authoritative control of anyone over anybody. Love for others, service to others, and esteeming others "as better than ourselves" is a rule of thumb for New Covenant Christianity, not the exception to it.

The state requires a "license" for performing weddings, and the 501C-3 non-profit must license its pastors for the state's recognition. I think it is a responsible act by a church body to license a minister to abide by state regulations, examining the candidate for the character traits outlined by Paul to young Timothy. However, any "licensed" minister – whether male or female – should be taught by the church body to never become infatuated with an unbiblical desire to have "authority over" other Christians.

Chapter 14: Service to Others Without Authority Over Others

If a person within a local church were to ever assume authority *over others* because of a position granted by the church, then Christ's authority of His people is being usurped.

There is only one Lord, Jesus Christ. And we who follow Him, as we live our lives "speaking the truth in love, we will grow to become in every respect *the mature body of Him who is the head*, that is, Christ" (Ephesians 4:15).

A believer should concern himself with loving others and serving others, and never be concerned with "authority over others." That's Christ's job.

If a church or convention were to ever believes that a person *automatically possesses spiritual authority* because of a position that the church has bestowed, then there is the danger of missing out on thrills and joys of seeing God's kingdom expanded on earth because *we begin to exclude or discount the ministries of God-called and Spirit-gifted people* who are not "office holders" of that church or denomination.

Christians infatuated with institutional church authority often miss the blessings that come from everyday Christians serving and ministering to others as the Kingdom of Christ is being built.

When the church sees those with spiritual authority as only those "ordained" to an office, then we've overlooked the New Covenant truth that the only one with authority over anyone is Jesus Christ, the head over us all.

FRAUDULENT AUTHORITY

The New Testament never teaches that there is some mystical "office" in the church with inherent authority for those who hold the office. The people of Christ are to recognize the gifts God has given his people, examine their lives for love and humility, and allow the Spirit to work through those gifted and called people as Christ adds to His church and builds His Kingdom.

The New Covenant people of God are particularly bound to the New Covenant (Testament) writings since the Old Covenant has been fulfilled by Christ and done away with (Hebrews 1:2, Acts 18:28).

For those who struggle with the phrase 'done away with,' the New Testament uses even sharper language like 'abolished.' This is why we do not offer sacrifices, celebrate the seven Jewish festivals, follow the Jewish dietary laws, etc.

Whereas in the Old Covenant you had it made if you were an old, Jewish male holding the office of priest or king (which was a legitimate office), in the New Covenant, all believers in Christ - both male and female, young and old, rich and poor, Greek and Jew - are priests and kings (co-heirs with Christ).

Christ is our Head; we are His Body. He is the King of kings; we are His servants.

New Covenant believers are responsible to the Head individually, but we also have a responsibility to fulfill in terms of each other (Rom. 14:4, Eph. 5:21).

All believers, not just men, are priests and servants of God.

All believers, not just men, are gifted by God.

All believers, not just men, are under the authority of the Head of the Body, Jesus Christ.

Therefore, we must all take our place among the Body to minister according to the gifts He has given us for the good of us all (1 Corinthians 12-14). It is God who gives us believers spiritual gifts to minister, and it is Christ the Head to whom we answer in the use of those gifts.

There are certain members of the body, both men and women, who become a gift to the body of Christ in unique ways. God has gifted and given these people to the body to equip all the members of the church for ministry (Ephesians 4:11-12).

When the New Testament describes these individuals, no emphasis is placed on any "authority" they possess that is derived from any "office" they hold. Rather, the people of God in the church have observed the Kingdom advanced through the servant leadership of those gifted individuals.

It is not the 'office' of pastor that bestows any power, but Christ who empowers the servant leadership.

Part of the confusion in the minds of some Southern Baptists over this issue may arise from the King James Version translating the word *'diakonia'* in Romans 11:13 with the word
'office.'

Unfortunately, the KJV translation is a poor one, simply because *'diakonia'* means *"service or ministry."*

This is important. So, let me show you again the difference between a service and an office, and why authority arises

FRAUDULENT AUTHORITY

from service and not an office. When Paul, a Jew, desired for the Gentiles to listen to his teaching, he reminds them of his ministry or service to them - not any imagined office of authority.

Some evangelicals think there is something mystical about a pastor and his inherent authority. Because of the "office" the pastor holds, people ought to listen to Him. That's not the way it was, however, even in Paul's day. The Bereans, Christians of "noble character," heard Paul and didn't accept what he said as true because Paul said it. Rather, they "examined the Scriptures with great eagerness to see whether what Paul was saying was true" (Acts 17:11).

Any pastor who puts the emphasis on the "office" of the pastor and tells the congregation that they must listen because of his authority over them, is conducting his ministry in a manner contrary to the teachings of the New Testament.

The practice of the Apostle Paul and other leaders of the early church, not to mention the teachings of Christ about leadership, is completely contrary to any pastor exerting "authority" over anyone. Christ alone has authority over His people.

But what about Romans 11:13? It seems like Paul magnifies "his office" in that verse.

Here's the verse from the King James Version. Paul is speaking. *"For I speak to you Gentiles, inasmuch as I am the apostle of the Gentiles, I magnify mine office"* (Romans 11:13).

The word "office" in the KJV is a Greek word that should be translated "ministry" or "service."

FRAUDULENT AUTHORITY

Paul is reminding the Gentiles that his message ought to be heeded because of his *ministry* and *service* among them.

Under great persecution, with nothing to personally gain, this Jewish man named Paul put his life on the line at the hands of his own people (the Jews) in order to serve and minister to the Gentiles.

The English Standard Version translates **Romans 11:13** this way:

> "*I am speaking to you Gentiles, since* (**I have been sent**) *to the Gentiles, I magnify my ministry* (**to you**).

He is not saying his "office" gives him authority. That's not the New Covenant way.

While it is true that in the Old Covenant, the concept of 'the office' of the priest is a position of authority, in the New Covenant Scriptures, the Greek words that would imply some official "office" for the church are never used.

For instance, in **Romans 12:4** the King James poorly translates the Greek word "praxis" this way: *"For as we have many members in one body, and all members have not the same **office**."*

The Greek word *praxis* nowhere means *'office,'* but rather speaks of or one's *action* or *function*.

The English Standard Version correctly translates Romans 12:4 this way: *"For as in one body we have many members, and the members do not all have the same **function**."*

FRAUDULENT AUTHORITY

In other words, we do not all minister in the same way. We do not all serve in the same manner. "Function" has nothing to do with an "office of authority" in a church.

One of the biggest mistranslations and misunderstood verses is **1 Timothy 3:1**: "If a man aspires to the office of a bishop, he desires a noble task" (ESV).

The word *office is* nowhere in the original text. Let me say that again. The word 'office' isn't in I Timothy 3:1

The original Greek literally says, *"if anyone aspires to oversight (episkope), he desires a noble task"* The sacred text speaks of one aspiring to a ministry of service, not a mystical office of authority.

Authority is to be experienced in the assembly because of the gifts and ministries of the Holy Spirit obvious in those believers who persuade others by their character and example.

In one sense, the entire body shares authority (Ephesians 5:21, 1 Peter 5:5), but in another sense, there are times when we recognize one another's gifts, knowledge, or experiences in the Lord and we choose to follow their lead. Our submission to another believer's servant leadership is because we see evidence that the Holy Spirit has empowered them with special gifts and that the Spirit has anointed their ministry or service through their humble, gracious, unselfish character.

My father, Paul Burleson, clearly articulates that this is the key to understanding the authority of anyone who ministers in the local church or is sent by the church to minister to others. He writes: "No one has authority because they have a stronger personality, knows more Bible, or they hold an office. That is foreign to the New Testament. Paul the Apostle had to defend his Apostleship by virtue of it being the work of the Spirit setting him aside for it. 1 Timothy 5:17 speaks of those elders that "give oversight well" and "are worthy of double honor."

It is the "giving (of) oversight well" that is the source of their ability to lead others in the church.

"Giving oversight well" is a gift of the Holy Spirit's anointing.

In other words, the anointing of the Spirit makes clear the authority that rests on a ministry done well. We are to follow anointed leadership. We don't follow someone because they hold an "alleged office" of authority.

There must be proof that the Spirit has gifted and anointed the leader before we choose to follow.

That's biblical.

That's logical.

That's practical.

FRAUDULENT AUTHORITY

Chapter 15: Illustrating Anointed Female Ministry

Servanthood is the badge of genuine Christian living.

Service to others that flows out of love for others is to be the overriding characteristic of whether or not someone is a follower of Jesus – a true minister of the gospel to others.

Josephine Scaggs was a female missionary to Africa working under the auspices of the Foreign Mission Board of the Southern Baptist Convention.

She was the first white woman to actually go to the jungles of Nigeria and establish a Christian church. She also founded a pastor's school and a medical clinic. Jo had to get permission from both the British government and the Foreign Mission Board to go to Nigeria.

When the Foreign Mission Board initially refused, she said she was going to resign and go anyway because her ultimate authority, Jesus Christ, had told her to go.

The Board relented, and it was a good thing.

This Southern Baptist woman led thousands of people to Christ, baptized them, and then taught and trained them herself. All told, Josephine Skaggs led 1700 of her converts to become Christian pastors.

During one of our Southern Baptist Conventions in the 1950s, Josephine stood before the Convention during the Foreign

FRAUDULENT AUTHORITY

Mission Board report and preached to the messengers on their sin of racism.

She asked why they would send her and other missionaries to Africa to share the Good News with black men and women, but Southern Baptist Pastors would not allow them in their churches.

This was the same year that W.A. Criswell, who occupied the 'office' of pastor at First Baptist Church, Dallas, Texas, delivered a message praising segregation and calling anyone who proposed desegregation 'heretics.'

Dr. Criswell later repented and confessed his sin by saying "Never have I been so blind."

This anecdote illustrates the difference between the authority of ministry and the authority of an office.

Besides Josephine Skaggs, Southern Baptists have had women like Lottie Moon and Bertha Smith, women whom leaders of the Conservative Resurgence claim as some of their heroes. These women constantly ministered among men, taught men in seminary classes, preached behind the pulpits of some of our greatest Southern Baptist Churches, and led thousands of people to faith in Christ.

These women, were they alive today, would be faced with the horrible possibility of not even being recognized as true, gifted and powerful servants of God within their own convention.

Many evangelical leaders are in danger of losing sight of real Christianity and the ministry of God-called, Spirit-gifted, Christ honoring women. Evangelicalism has fallen into the

FRAUDULENT AUTHORITY

trap of believing there is something sacred and authoritative about an "office" of a pastor, rather than seeing New Testament Christianity as a body of people, both men and women, serving as gifted under the Headship of Christ.

The teaching of the infallible Word of God is that the real transformative power of Kingdom advancement comes from the love and service of the people of God, both men and women, as we are empowered and sent by Jesus Christ.

We are in danger as conservative, Bible-believing followers of Jesus Christ of losing sight of New Testament Christianity.

When we "ordain" only men to hold the 'office' of the pastor, and see these ordained men as having power and control "over others," we advocate a type of Christianity that is foreign to the New Testament. These ordained pastors are often allowed by their congregations to exert absolute authority over people because they are deemed the church's "spiritual authority."

This is simply not biblical.

Jesus Christ is our authority, and all men and women serve as He gifts us, under His Lordship. Conservative evangelicals are in confused when it comes to authority.

We are in danger of losing some of our most gifted, God-called, Christ-honoring women from our seminaries, colleges, churches, agencies, mission fields, and other places of service because we are refusing to follow the clear teaching of Scripture. *Real authority flows from gifted service as empowered by Christ* - and is not gender or office based within the church.

Chapter 16: Gifted Women Are Wrongly Excluded from Service

A few years ago, I became acquainted with an extraordinarily gifted follower of Jesus named Paige Heard. Paige was serving as a Regimental Army Chaplain at historic West Point Military Academy. Every Sunday Chaplain Heard could be heard preaching the gospel at 10:30 a.m. during the Protestant worship service at the beautiful West Point Military Academy Cadet Chapel.

Major Heard is a life-long Southern Baptist and a graduate of Dallas Theological Seminary and New Orleans Seminary.

She faithfully served Christ as a Southern Baptist-endorsed United States Army Chaplain beginning 1996. Paige is a conservative Christian. She believes the Bible is the infallible, inerrant, and sufficient Word of God.

At the time I became acquainted with her, she was only one of five female Southern Baptist chaplains left in the United States Army.

Eight years after Paige began serving our country as an Army Chaplain, the trustees of the North American Mission Board of the Southern Baptist Convention voted to stop endorsing female chaplains.

Major Heard had been endorsed before the 2004 prohibition and was 'grandfathered' in.

FRAUDULENT AUTHORITY

Paige told me via phone that her heart "ached for the Southern Baptist Convention and the stance her convention on gifted women serving.

On the one hand, Paige said, Southern Baptist churches are training girls in G.A's (Girls in Action) and Acteens that they are to listen to the voice and calling of God and serve Him. But when those same girls fulfill the call of God on their lives, the very Convention who trained them then turns their collective back on them.

Paige said that she is thoroughly Baptist in conviction and as conservative as a Christian can be regarding the fundamentals of the faith and views on the authority and sufficiency of Scripture.

She believes that conservative, gifted females who believe in Christ and His Word are being pushed out of the Southern Baptist Convention into more liberal denominations because of the unbiblical views on "women in ministry" that are being pushed by some Southern Baptists.

Paige grew up in Peachtree City, Georgia, a suburb of Atlanta and attended the First Baptist Church there. She was involved in G.A's, Acteens and as a young adult, Teen Missions International. She graduated from Auburn University and afterwards obtained her Master of Biblical Arts at Dallas Theological Seminary.

Paige attended DTS seminary to fulfill the education requirements for her calling as a chaplain. When she applied for the position as chaplain at a women's prison, the state of Georgia informed her that her home church needed to ordain her to meet the job qualifications. In 1989 the First Baptist Church of Peachtree City, Georgia, ordained Paige.

When members of the congregation asked about the appropriateness of 'ordaining' a female, the pastor responded that the church was acknowledging the calling and gifts of a young lady they had known for more than two decades. Further, *since 'ordination' is nowhere mentioned in Scripture*, they would simply lay their hands on their member to set her apart to fulfill the call of God on her life - and that would suffice to meet the requirements of the state for her to obtain the job at the women's prison.

Five families left the church, but the majority of the conservative members supported the decision to set aside Paige Heard to Chaplain Ministry.

Paige served as a Georgia State Prison Chaplain from 1990-1992, and then enrolled in New Orleans Seminary to obtain her Master of Divinity Degree. In 1996 Paige joined the United States Army and had served the past ten years in active duty.

The North American Mission Board-endorsed Paige in 1996 as a chaplain for the U.S. Army. The trustees of the North American Mission Board voted in 2004 to stop endorsing female chaplains. As a result, there are only five women chaplains affiliated with the Southern Baptist Convention who remain in the United States Army, including Paige.

It is interesting to note that the North American Mission Board had initially said they would not appoint 'ordained' women. But when they learned that the Army did not require ordination for a woman to serve as Chaplain, just an endorsement from NAMB, the trustees scrambled to stop the practice of endorsements in 2004.

In explaining "why," the trustees would no longer endorse 'women' to be chaplains for the Army, the NAMB Chairman

FRAUDULENT AUTHORITY

of the Trustee Board said, "we will not endorse a woman where the role and function of the chaplain would be seen the same as that of a pastor."

What is harmful about a woman being in a role that is "seen the same as that of a pastor?"

It has to do with authority.

Men, according to the bizarre views of authority to which some evangelicals hold, have "it" (e.g., authority), but women can't have "it."

It could be argued that Chaplain Heard does not occupy the "office of pastor." But that misses the point that the "office of pastor is not biblical." The *function and servant ministry* of a pastor is biblical, and it is quite certain that Paige fulfills the function of a pastor while carrying out her duties as a chaplain for the United States Army.

Paige faithfully proclaims the gospel every Sunday during the Protestant chapel service.

Paige has had the privilege of leading over thirty men and women to faith in Christ during the past year and has baptized them all - some in makeshift baptisteries in the deserts of Iraq.

Paige administers the Lord's Supper and has performed wedding ceremonies, conducted funerals and provided encouragement and counseling to troops. She is highly respected among the troops. In fact, there are dozens upon dozens of individuals and families whose lives have been transformed by Southern Baptist Paige Heard fulfilling her calling as a chaplain to the United States Army.

FRAUDULENT AUTHORITY

One young male Southern Baptist pastor recently told me that any female who functions in the role of a pastor is in 'rebellion to God.'

The Bible compares rebellion to witchcraft (I Sam. 15:23).

I served for over a decade on a law enforcement task force that investigated crimes that involved the occult, including that of witchcraft, satanism, and shamanism. I can say without equivocation that I've seen the black arts up close.

To call a woman ministering the gospel of Jesus Christ, by the power of the Spirit, a person who is in 'rebellion to God' is an offense to those of us who understand what true rebellion to God is all about.

I imagine it is also an offense to those whose lives who have been transformed through the ministry of Southern Baptist United States Army Chaplain Paige Heard.

Chapter 17: Moving Away from Male Spiritual Authority

The following is a transcript of a message I preached in Norman, Oklahoma, on Friday, August 7, 2009. It was originally titled "By Our Love Shall All People Know We Are His Disciples." It was my goal to lay out my journey away from a belief that males were to "rule over" their families, churches and other people because males had inherent "spiritual authority."

I'd been taught that by those I respected. But I've since come to a conclusion through reading the New Testament that this belief in inherent male authority is antithetical to the teachings of the New Testament and the practice of Jesus Christ.

I would ask that you carefully read why I've come to see the New Covenant truth of the equality of the body of Christ under the headship of Christ.

"Shortly before His betrayal, Jesus gathered His disciples around him and said, *"A new commandment I give to you, that you love one another, even as I have loved you, that you also love one another. By* (your love for one another) *all people will know that you are my disciples"* (John 13:34-35).

On July 4th, 2009, Baptist pastor Rick Warren spoke at the 2009 Islamic Society of North America Conference in our nation's capital. Over 40,000 Islamic believers gathered in Washington D.C. for this conference, considered to be the largest annual gathering of Muslim Americans. Pastor

FRAUDULENT AUTHORITY

Warren challenged the gathered Muslims to join Christians in modeling for the world what it means to:

First, respect the dignity of every person by not merely tolerating people but valuing them.

Second, restore civility to civilization by disagreeing without being disagreeable, and

Third, reinforce the protection of the freedoms of speech and religion for every individual within our respective cultures.

Warren proposed that in this very diverse world when Christians and Muslims model this mutual respect and love for each other while protecting the freedoms of the individual, an even greater common good will arise—peace. Warren pointed to the 60,000 different kinds of beetles as evidence that the God of all peace loves diversity.

As for me, I believe that God's love for diversity is irrefutably proven by the 60,000 different kinds of Baptists God has created.

Rick Warren--a family friend since the late 1970s when he attended Southcliff Baptist Church, a church which at the time was pastored by my father--acquitted himself and all evangelicals quite well in his speech before those 40,000 Muslims. Some Baptists have expressed surprise that the Muslims issued Rick an invitation to speak. Other Baptists have expressed regret that he accepted.

My disappointment is that the different kinds of Baptists like those of us represented here at the New Baptist Covenant

FRAUDULENT AUTHORITY

Conference, and others who are not here, were not in the audience in Washington D.C. to hear the speech ourselves.

For it seems to me that we Baptists can never really value Muslims, treat them with civility, or grant them the freedom to speak and believe as they see fit until we first learn to treat our different kinds of Baptist brothers and sisters around the world in the same manner.

In other words, until I can treat all my Baptist friends with dignity, value them as people, and respect their views--particularly and especially those Baptists who disagree with me- -it will be impossible for me to treat Muslims in the same manner.

Likewise, until my liberal or moderate Baptist friends experience Christ's love in their hearts for me, a theologically conservative Baptist, and until they value my personhood, respect my views, and work with me toward a greater common good, it will be impossible for them to do the same for Muslims.

The greatest barometer for how well we Baptists understand the importance of agape love, which Scriptures call the distinguishing mark of followers of Jesus Christ, is our treatment of each other.

This evening I would like to make a personal confession to you, my Baptist brothers and sisters, who do not see eye to eye with me either theologically, socially, morally, spiritually or politically. I come from a long line of Baptist preachers. The Burleson family settled in Texas with one ancestor, Dr. Rufus Burleson, becoming the first President of Baylor University. My branch of the Burlesons moved to Oklahoma at the turn of this century, and several of the Burlesons would eventually become pastors or missionaries.

We like to talk about the Baptists in our family, but don't often mention the Burleson who is the only person to ever escape from Alcatraz (smile). I have served two terms as President of the Baptist General Convention of Oklahoma, and now I pastor a large church in northwestern Oklahoma.
   Tonight I speak for myself only. My confession and corresponding repentance is personal, spoken with a heart that genuinely desires to do my part of building bridges between all Baptists who name Christ as Lord.

The people I pastor know what kind of Baptist I am--Calvinistic in my soteriology, partial-preterist in my eschatology, open communion in my ecclesiology, conservative in my theology, inerrantist in my bibliology, and continuationist in my pneumatology--(I know that sounds like a medical diagnosis, but they are the proper labels for my theological views). I held these views when I began pastoring over a quarter of a century ago, and I hold to them unto this day.

I have not changed what I believe, but I myself have changed in one very critical area over the past few years.

I now believe deep in my heart that Jesus is more concerned with how we Baptists treat each other than He is what we Baptists teach each other. The people loved by Christ--particularly those who differ with me--are to be far more precious to me than any finer point of theology believed by me. Jesus did not tell me that it would be by my "truth" that all people would know that I am one of His followers, but by my "love." The only description that is ever given of our Lord was that He was a person "full of grace and truth."

FRAUDULENT AUTHORITY

Word order is important in Scripture. Grace should not just precede truth; it should permeate it. Or as our host Jimmy Allen so brilliantly puts it: "Our love should reach beyond our theology."

A few years ago, Pastor Julie Pennington Russell held the hand of her seven-year-old son Taylor as she walked through the picket lines that had formed outside Calvary Baptist Church, Waco, Texas. The picketers, Baptists from surrounding churches, were there protesting Julie's call to become the pastor of Calvary. As she walked through the picket line her little boy squeezed her hand, pulled his mother down where she could hear, and then asked, "Mommy, who is Jezebel and why are they calling you that?"

It has been said that when the old Irish immersed a babe at baptism, they would leave out the babe's right arm so that it would remain "pagan for good fighting." I have sometimes wondered if it is our custom as Baptists to plunge all but the convert's mouth into the baptismal waters to keep the Baptist tongue "pagan for good fighting."

I confess that in years past, it has been easier for me to stand behind a principle and say something negative about the character of those who disagree with me than to simply love my fellow Baptists who do not see eye to eye with me theologically.

I have not changed what I believe, nor have I moved away from a conservative view of the infallible sacred text, but what has changed is the need to point out that people who disagree with in interpretations of the Bible are less Christian, less "spiritual," less loved by God than I.

This is simply not true. The love of God for His people never changes or wanes, regardless of our actual or imagined theological unfaithfulness. Or perhaps it should be stated by me more precisely. God's love for His people never wanes or abates regardless of my fellow Baptists actual or imagined theological unfaithfulness. Jesus warned us that we tend to focus on the speck in our brother's eye while ignoring the plank in our own.

I am now committed to follow the commandment of my Lord and to display total and unconditional grace, kindness and love to all my Baptist brothers and sisters in Christ, regardless of our theological differences. You are more important to me – more so than even my principles—and this is both biblical and Christian. To me, this is the peculiar mark of real, genuine Christianity.

This, of course, does not mean that we should not speak out when we perceive an injustice against God's people. It is often the wise and prudent course to graciously keep silent when we hear fellow Christians voice interpretations of Scripture that are contrary to our own interpretations, knowing that we are fallible people dealing with a sacred text.

But when a fellow human being, ESPECIALLY a believer in Christ, is personally being abused or mistreated, our silence or non- action can never be justified or condoned by Christ and His sacred command to love one another.

Those who risk everything to correct injustices against Christ's people, who diligently protect the powerless in God's kingdom, who defend the downtrodden in this world, who rescue the abused, and who care for the needy are expressing the love that Christ mentions as the peculiar mark of His followers.

FRAUDULENT AUTHORITY

It has come to my attention these past few years that my sisters in Christ within the Baptist faith are often in need of such defense. The parallels between the modern American Baptist woman and the 19th century American Baptist black are numerous. To defend a gifted Baptist woman today is considered by some Baptist men as an unbiblical act.

To call any mistreatment of Baptist women today "un-Christian" is tantamount to treason in the eyes of some Baptist leaders. Many Baptists believe, particularly in the Southern Baptist Convention, that to defend Baptist women and to attempt to set them free to serve to the full extent of God's call and giftedness in their lives is a denial of the faith.

But I propose that any action taken to prevent the mistreatment of Baptist women in ministry is the most loving thing that can be done to both the victim and the one who is oppressing. In my opinion, the protection of Baptist women who minister to others is the fulfillment of Christ's biblical command to love each other as Christ has loved us.

In 2004 Dr. Sheri Klouda was terminated from Southwestern Baptist Theological Seminary's faculty as the distinguished professor of Hebrew because the seminary's new male administration held to a principle that a "woman should never teach a man." Sheri was released from the job of her dreams and forced to relocate to Indiana, taking a far less paying position at a Christian college. Sheri's husband, Pinky, whom administration knew was suffering from critical cardiac problems at the time, had to leave his medical care in Fort Worth because of the forced relocation.

Sheri's daughter also had to leave her much beloved high school where she was to graduate the very next year. Sheri and her family were forced from a house in Fort Worth that they had purchased just a few months earlier—all because of administration following a perceived "theological principle."

When our church contacted Sheri a few months after her termination, we discovered she was selling pints of her own blood to help meet medical expenses for her husband. Regardless of one's views regarding women "teaching" men at Baptist seminaries, the question Baptists face is whether or not the treatment of Sheri Klouda fulfills Christ's commandment that we love one another as Christ has loved us. If it does not, then something must be done.

The God who shed his blood for us would not want us turning a blind eye to His people selling their own blood for the sake of others. Over several months our church helped raise over $20,000 dollars for the Klouda family. Christ's command to love one another precludes silence or indifference when injustices occur. We are not even allowed by our Lord to hide behind our principles when it comes to loving His people. Our love should reach beyond our theology.

For this reason, it seems to me that if we Baptists are serious about loving one another in the manner that Christ has loved us, then we cannot, we must not, remain quiet or silent when we see our Baptist sisters in Christ suffer. Baptist women in ministry, believers like Sarah Stewart, from whom we heard a testimony tonight, are women we are called to love, support and protect.

These women profess a call from God, show real evidence of being set apart by Christ, and have experienced the empowerment of the Holy Spirit to proclaim Jesus Christ and Him crucified to the world—yet many of them are being subjected to abuse, and that by Baptists. When our Baptist women in ministry experience such personal mistreatment,

FRAUDULENT AUTHORITY

ridicule or harm, we are commanded by Christ our Lord to bind up their wounds—and sometimes we must even take the weapon of abuse out of the hands of the perpetrators of those wounds.

In 2004, during the last business session which I moderated at the Baptist General Convention of Oklahoma, an extraordinary, godly woman from Quail Springs Baptist Church, OKC was elected second vice-president. I will never forget the sight from the platform as several men throughout the auditorium stood and literally turned their backs to the platform as they voted "against" the first woman to be elected to general office within the Baptist General Convention of Oklahoma. That moment was an awakening for me.

I realized that any cherished principle that would ever CAUSE a Christian to be uncivil, unkind or unloving toward a sister in Christ is a principle that should be thrown out for the sake of obedience to the command of Christ to love one another. I am not offended by those who wish to argue with me over this point for your argument is not ultimately with me, but with Jesus Christ. It is His command, not mine.

History will one day look back on how we Baptists in the 21st century treated our women who were called by God to minister. It is my prayer that conservative, Bible believing men will not make the same mistake our Southern Baptist forefathers made when they remained quiet two centuries ago as another minority experienced abuse. The ground at the foot of the cross is level so that there is no supremacy of whites, no supremacy of males, and no supremacy of the rich--the wall of partition has been removed, and we are called to love every believer in Christ the way Christ loves us.

FRAUDULENT AUTHORITY

I will never forget the email I received from one of the young ladies in our Baptist seminaries who wrote me, confiding that she typed with tears in her eyes, having just come from her "preaching class" where the professor allowed all the "men and boys" in the class to remove themselves from the room so they would not be subjected to hearing a woman teach the Word of God. The young lady found herself preaching to the walls and wondered whether or not she had a place in Baptist life.

I reminded the young lady that she was not preaching to the walls, but to the Father, the Son, and the Spirit who were One in her midst as she preached. The prophet declares that God sings over His people with joy (Zephaniah 3:17) and I guaranteed her that the Father sings all the louder over a woman who unashamedly and boldly declares the glories of His Son!

One of these days we Baptists will get to the place when we realize that publicly censoring women preachers like Julie Pennington, firing Baptist women professors like Sheri Klouda, walking out on women preachers like that young seminary student, or turning our back on women Baptist leaders--acting as if women don't have a place in the kingdom of God--says more about our lack of love and grace toward all the followers of Jesus Christ and our own disobedience to Christ's great commandment than it does our "love for truth."

Last week National Public Radio religion editor Barbara Bradley- Hagerty interviewed me for a piece she was doing entitled "Baptist Leaders Face Challenge On Women's Roles." She quotes me in the radio interview saying "Jesus treated women as equals" and that I believe "there is a quiet underground movement within the convention to rethink

FRAUDULENT AUTHORITY

women's roles." After my quote, you can hear slow laughing from a deep voice in the background—"*Ha..Ha..Ha...*"

It was the Director of the Southern Baptist Ethics and Religious Liberty Commission in Washington D.C. He then tells the radio audience, "Burleson is dreaming." I reflected on this the Director's statement. He is a brilliant man, capable of playing three-dimensional chess and formulating his rationale with cogent logic. He, like I, believes in an inerrant Bible. Upon reflection of his statement that I was dreaming, I came to the conclusion that he is right. "I have a dream . . ."

I have a dream that a woman like Wendy Norvelle, former acting Vice-President of the International Mission Board, will be promoted to a permanent position of leadership among Baptists because of her qualifications and gifts—and not barred from promotion because of her gender.

I have a dream that a Southern Baptist woman like Major Paige Heard, the Regimental Army Chaplain at the historic West Point Military Academy, will be heard preaching the gospel at 10:30 a.m. every Sunday at the historic Cadet Chapel and we Baptists will all know and believe that Major Heard is honoring Christ in her proclamation of the gospel and be proud to call her one of our Baptist chaplains.

I have a dream that Baptists will one day make much over the gospel that women like Sarah Stewart preach and absolutely nothing over the gender they possess.

I have a dream that unlike slavery in the 1800s, Baptists in the south will realize the Bible speaks against patriarchal homes where wives are slaves to their husbands, autocratic churches where women are servants to leaders, and authoritarian societies where women are subservient to men.

I have a dream that young women in our Baptist Conventions can follow great women missionaries of the past and travel overseas to share the gospel with both men and women, baptizing converts in the name of Jesus Christ and nurturing them in the ways of Scripture–- just as Lottie Moon did over 150 years ago.

If some Baptists would say to me that my dream is simply capitulation to the agenda of radical feminists, I respond with loving, but firm words: "No, setting Baptist women free to serve is not relenting to societal or cultural pressures, but rather, it is fulfillment of the commandment of Christ Jesus Himself."

Regardless of whether or not my fellow Baptist conservatives agree with what I believe the Bible teaches regarding the real equality of women in Christ's kingdom, there is no wiggle room when it comes to the commandment of our Lord. Every Baptist is obligated to love our Baptist women as Jesus has loved us.

I do not know of one time when Christ has ever withheld from me any good gift, has stifled my expression of any praise of Him, or shut me up from proclaiming His Word – so logically His commandment to love my sisters in Christ as He has loved me should negate any and every attempt to withhold from our faith community a Baptist woman gifted by Christ.

Our obedience to His command should preclude any attempt to stifle a Baptist woman compelled to publicly praise Jesus Christ.

FRAUDULENT AUTHORITY

It should lead us to resist any effort to shut up or censor any Baptist woman called to preach Christ and Him crucified. It is impossible for my Baptist brothers to point to any text – let me repeat this—it is impossible for my Baptist brothers to point to any text, which is properly understood in its context, that compels Baptist men to suppress Baptist women in terms of ministry. On the contrary, we are called by our Lord to support and love those women of faith just as our Lord has loved us.

Black Mesa is in the far northwestern edge of Oklahoma's panhandle. Its summit is 4,972.9 feet above sea level, just under a football field of being one mile high. It is the highest point of elevation in Oklahoma. People come from all over the world to observe the stars that "kiss your nose" at night on Black Mesa. This past June, on a sunny afternoon, I hiked to the top of Black Mesa. As I rested and reflected on the plateau before my descent, my eye caught a passenger jet flying east to west above me. I could clearly see the plane's fuselage and the long, white crystallized cloud the jet formed as it crossed the blue sky. I thought about the couple of hundred passengers heading west.

Then I looked down and saw a Burlington Northern - Santa Fe train snaking its way west as well. Beside the train was a modern state highway where a handful of cars were also heading west. Just a few miles south of the railroad tracks and the highway, easily seen from my position on Black Mesa, was the Old Santa Fe Trail (Cimarron Cutoff). Most travelers and traders heading west in the 1800s took this trail by horseback, wagon or foot. As I was thinking about all this, I pulled out my Blackberry Curve and saw that I had missed a couple of calls.

And then it hit me. For the past 200 years, the mission of every person who traversed the land before me was simple—

FRAUDULENT AUTHORITY

go west. Their mission never changed and was the same—west, west, go west! But the methodology of going west has changed over the years – from foot to horse, to wagon, to train, to car to plane! How foolish would it be for someone today to use the same methodology that was being used in the 1820s to fulfill the mission of heading west?

For Baptists, our mission has not changed for the past 200 years—-nay, for the past 2000 years. Our mission is to proclaim Jesus, to preach Jesus, to publicize Jesus, to present Jesus, to give Jesus to a lost and dying world. Our mission is all about the story of Jesus. Men and women of faith are called by the One who commissioned us to support and love one another as we seek to fulfill that mission.

It is time we Baptists see that the methodology by which we share Jesus must change, or we will die a slow death without ever accomplishing our mission. Whenever institutions crystallize their methodologies rather than their mission, the institution becomes brittle and dies.

Jesus commands us to love each other—love those different from us, love those on mission with us, love each and every follower of Jesus. How we fulfill our mission will continually change. The walls are down. Our methodologies should be fluid, but our mission shall never change.

You may not like the fact that women are now being called by God to preach, or called by God to do missions, or called by God to teach. You may even consider it a violation of your principles for a woman to teach a man, or preach Christ to a man, or baptize a man, or lead a man, but there is one thing that you and I cannot--we must not--forget.

You and I are called to love each and every sister in Christ who feels called to ministry. We are called to affirm the

FRAUDULENT AUTHORITY

dignity of every Christian woman called to minister. We are commanded to treat them with respect and civility. We are also called to love, respect and affirm the autonomy of local Baptist congregations and denominations that utilize these gifted women in ministry as they see fit.

To censor them, reject them, abuse them or condemn their character is a sin of the first order.

The principles Rick Warren gave to the Muslims one month ago are just as relevant to all us Baptists today and for the years to come. The only way we will ever have peace between Christians and the Muslims in this world is when we Baptists first begin to value the dignity of our sisters in Christ who are called to minister, to respect those churches that call them to serve, and to protect the individual freedoms of our fellow Baptists to think, believe and act as their conscience leads them in obedience to Christ and His Word.

It is only then that we will display the kind love that Jesus says will distinguish us from the rest of the world.

May the God of all peace give us the grace to live in this manner before all people for Christ's sake. Amen."

Chapter 18: The Bizarre Practices of Those Who Believe in Male Authority

There is a young, Bible-believing pastor named J.D. Greear. J.D. is pastor of The Summit Church in Raleigh/Durham North Carolina. He seems to be a visionary leader, and he has led Summit in a gospel centered approach to missions and church planting.

However, J.D.'s view on women and so-called "spiritual authority" is quite typical among conservative evangelicals, but bizarre in practice and antithetical to the teachings of the New Testament.

In May of 2015, J.D. Greear had a woman named Elyse Fitspatrick "speak" at *The Summit* on Sunday morning. Elyse is the author of several books, and according to J.D. Greear, is his wife's "favorite Bible teacher."

J.D. should be commended for having Elyse speak on Mother's Day, 2015. It seems, however, that this invitation caused some consternation at Summit. 10 days after Elyse spoke, J.D. wrote a blog post entitled *Can Women Teach in the Church?* He writes: "Our elders have been working on a statement explaining the roles God has given to women in the ministries of our church. That statement is still in the works, but our recent invitation to have Elyse Fitzpatrick share during weekend services has led some to ask whether we believe a woman can preach and teach in the mixed-gender gathering of the church."

FRAUDULENT AUTHORITY

J.D. then attempts to answer that question by quoting I Timothy 2 and John Piper. J.D. concludes:

"In context, I think [1 Tim 2:12] means that women shouldn't be the **authoritative teachers** of the church..."

J.D. goes on to define what "authoritative teaching" means: **"Authoritative teaching"** in a church is (1) teaching that is binding for that particular congregation and (2) the teaching that comprises that church's fulfillment of its responsibility to pass on the faith to the next generation. J.D. said the elders have the "authority" to teach official doctrine and remove those from membership who disagree.

Elyse Fitspatrick couldn't officially "teach" anyone at The Summit, because she was without "authority."

J.D's teaching on "authoritative teaching" is absurd. There are two biblical reasons I say this:

1. **The authority behind Truth is always the greatness of the message, not the genitalia of the messenger.**

"For I am not ashamed of the gospel, because it (e.g. "the gospel" not the "messenger") is the power of God that brings deliverance to everyone who believes: first to the Jew, then to the Gentile." (Romans 1:16).

If God spoke truth to Balaam through an ass, He could surely speak authoritative Truth to the world through men and women. Jesus Christ said, "I am the Way, the Truth, and the Life," He is the Truth; and if He is the topic of the message, the authority of the message comes from Him, not the messenger.

FRAUDULENT AUTHORITY

2. If you wrongly believe that there is an inherent authority in males, then you must treat female messengers of the powerful gospel differently.

This is where it gets weird.

To show how a woman speaking "truth" at the Summit is one without authority, J.D. sets up a "hedge of protection" for the congregation lest they perceive (his word, not mine), that the woman has authority when she does not.

He writes: "A woman can teach in a large formal setting, like a mixed Sunday School class or an evening Bible study, but she must not do so in a way that "mimics" the teaching authority of a male elder. Perceptions are important, and if some in the church begin to look to a woman-teacher as their primary shepherd-leader, both she and they have gone into error."

Wow.

But what about Elyse Fitzpatrick?

She spoke on a Sunday morning during the "sermon time" at Summit. J.D. explains how he and the males at Summit took several steps to prevent the wrong perception that Elyse had some authority over the congregation.

J.D. writes: "A teaching elder at Summit (e.g., J.D.) set the context, invited Elyse up to ask her a series of questions, and then (I) wrapped up the service by applying her words specifically to The Summit Church. The elder's introduction, presence on stage, and application at the end "officialized" the explanation and exhortation given by her for The Summit Church, and made clear she was not teaching (as one with authority) in our church. She explained the content, but we,

FRAUDULENT AUTHORITY

the Summit elders, bore the weight of responsibility for teaching."

If you watch Elyse Fitzpatrick's message on Sunday morning at *The Summit*, you will notice she was not allowed things that other male speakers can do at *The Summit*. For example:

1). Elyse could not stand as she taught, she had to sit, lest it is perceived she had authority.

2). Elyse could not "declare" truth; she had to be asked questions from one in authority.

3). Elyse could not "apply" the Truth to the congregation; only those with authority could do this.

4). Elyse had to be "introduced" and "followed-up" by a male with authority.

5). Had Elyse Fitzpatrick spoken the truth the way males usually do at Summit, there would have been shock among the Summit men.

When evangelical churches like The Summit promote as "biblical and normal" male authority over females, then evangelicals will have far more in common with Muslim culture and the Muslim religion than we ever will with the Good News of Jesus Christ.

The gospel, the New Testament, the New Covenant shed in His blood, and the Messiah Himself elevated women to equal status in the Kingdom of God. Equal does not mean identical. Men and women in the Kingdom of God are different, but men and women in the Kingdom of God are equal. There is equal worth (in Christ), equal significance (born of the Spirit),

FRAUDULENT AUTHORITY

equal authority (we are all "priests unto God"), equal inheritance (co- heirs with Christ), and equal value ("we are the blood-bought redeemed").

According to Greear, women who teach the Bible can't be in a position of declaring truth authoritatively, because nobody is to submit to a woman teaching the truth. Women are the acquiescers; males are the authoritarians. Males give; women receive. If a male receives "truth" from a woman, then "error" has a occurred because a male can't get anything authoritative from a woman.

There's a Greek word for such thinking - baloney.

At some point, evangelicals are going to need to wake-up to the New Covenant truth that Jesus Christ makes the ground at the foot of the cross equal.

Chapter 19: Only "That" Woman Should Be Quiet (I Timothy 2:11-15)

When the principles and practices of the kingdom of God are made subordinate to the traditions of men, the power of Spirit- filled living becomes a figment of our collective imagination. When religious leaders place shackles on God's people to keep them from functioning as He has gifted them to function, the church becomes a powerless shell of immobility.

Without the vivifying energy of the Spirit in the body of Christ, the King's men and women become regal attendants fighting at each rather than royal ambassadors working with each other. If you have ever experienced a dead church, you know intuitively that the deadness occurs because leadership is controlling guilty people rather than empowering gifted people.

The Scripture is emphatic that the Spirit gifts His people-- men and women--with gifts of teaching, service, leadership, mercy, organization, etc... Good leaders get to know their people, find out how they are gifted, and empower them to fulfill their calling.

The Bible is replete with examples of men and women gifted by God to teach and to lead. No Bible-believing Christian seems to have a problem with men leading or teaching, but women fulfilling those roles, as gifted by the Holy Spirit, seems to cause consternation in the lives of some who are more familiar with tradition than truth.

We have dozens of illustrations in the New Testament of women teaching men (Priscilla, Anna, Philip's four unmarried daughters, and many, many more). There are also dozens of additional illustrations in the Bible of women leading men.

I Timothy 2:11-15 Is the Text Used by Men to Restrict Gifted Women

Following is the text that is used to stifle women. I have placed only four words in (bold) that more accurately translate what Paul is saying, words that are a direct translation of the Greek.

The reasons for the four words I supply will be explained below: Paul says in I Timothy 2:11-15:

"Let a (the) woman learn in quietness and full submission. "12 I do not permit a (the) woman to teach or to assume authority over a (the) man; she must be quiet. 13 For Adam was formed first, then Eve. 14 And Adam was not the one deceived; it was the woman who was deceived and became a sinner. 15 But women (lit. "she") will be saved through childbearing—if they continue in faith, love and holiness with propriety."

The verses above seem to say, at least on the surface and without the four words I've supplied, that no woman should ever teach any man; that no woman should ever assume any 'authority' over any man; and that all women must always be quiet in the presence of men. Of course, most evangelical conservative men would say that the Apostle Paul was only addressing women "in the church" and "in the home" so that women in the political world, corporate world, and secular world, are not under these restrictions.

FRAUDULENT AUTHORITY

I find it humorous that evangelical conservatives complain of "potential malignancy" in one's gospel orthodoxy if one can find a way to make I Timothy 2 say that it is okay for women to teach men or have **authority over men** "in the church."

Why is that humorous to me? Because those same conservative men have already found a way (rightly so) to explain how a woman can have leadership over a man and teach a man in every other realm of life (politics, business, etc...). Do we remember when Condi Rice, Secretary of State, spoke to the Southern Baptist Convention?

She taught us Southern Baptist men a great deal about war and the bombing of terrorists, and we applauded her leadership as Secretary of State. So much for the gospel malignancy theory.

But back to the I Timothy 2 text above. For those of you "in the church" who get stuck on this text, and as a result, refuse to have women read the Bible in public at church, or teach a discipleship class with men in it, or refuse to have women serve as trustees, or elders, or committee chairpersons "in the church: lest they 'assume authority' over men, let me help you see how you are totally ignoring the clear teaching of the New Testament in favor of a poor and false interpretation of these I Timothy 2 verses.

For anyone who wants to make women in leadership an issue of gospel orthodoxy in the local church, I provide below a very clear interpretation of **I Timothy 2:11-15** that is consistent with the rest of the New Testament's teaching on empowering women in their giftedness. There are five basic principles that must be understood in order to rightly comprehend what Paul is saying:

(1). Paul is addressing a problem Timothy had with a specific woman teaching heresy to a specific man in the church at Ephesus.

How do we know this? There are at least four grammatical reasons:

a). Paul gives instructions to "women" (plural) at the beginning of chapter two (i.e., how to dress modestly, live of life of good works, etc...), but beginning with verse 11, Paul switches from the plural noun (women) to the singular noun (woman). The definitive article "the" is in the original Greek (i.e. "the woman"), not the unfortunate translation "a" woman (NIV; NASB). Paul moves from instructions to women in general (vs. 910) to very direct instructions for a specific woman in verse 11. You can verify this quite easily with any online interlinear.

b). The "she" in verse 15 is third person singular (again, the NIV and NASB, unfortunately, mistranslate the third person singular Greek pronoun in v. 15 with the plural English noun "women"). The "she" of verse 15 is the same woman in verse 11 and verse 12. She is the woman who needs correcting.

c). *"...if they continue"* (v.15). The word "they" is the accurate translation of the third person plural used by Paul. This plural pronoun identifies not only the woman doing the teaching but also the man whom she is deceiving ("the woman" and "the man" of v. 12).

d). The verb "continue" is in the aorist active subjunctive. This verb's tense confirms that the instructions Paul gives in vs. 11- 15 are designed for the woman and the man in question (v. 12), to two people who are alive at the time Paul is writing and not to those who are either dead or not yet born (i.e., Eve or women in general).

(2). The woman in question was teaching error out of her ignorance and should be shown mercy.

Mercy and love toward false teachers is one of the themes of letter we call I Timothy, particularly because the assembly at Ephesus was a church filled with people from pagan backgrounds: "As I urged you upon my departure for Macedonia, remain on at Ephesus so that you may instruct certain men not to teach strange doctrines, nor to pay attention to myths and endless genealogies, which give rise to mere speculation rather than furthering the administration of God which is by faith. But the goal of our instruction is love from a pure heart and a good conscience and a sincere faith" (I Timothy 1:3-5).

Paul had already spoken of the ignorance he was in before he was taught the truth: "(I) was a blasphemer, and a persecutor, and insolent; but I received mercy because being ignorant I did it in unbelief" (I Timothy 1:13).

Paul mentions how Eve sinned in ignorance: "...it was the woman (Eve) who was deceived and became a sinner" (I Timothy 2:13). The entire first two chapters of I Timothy are leading up to Paul expressing sympathy toward and encouraging Timothy to display love to, that woman teaching error.

We know that Paul wrote this letter in response to problems Timothy was facing in Ephesus, and those problems were known by Paul (I Timothy 3:14-15). This is a personal letter, not a general epistle, and proper interpretation requires the reader to delve into why Paul wrote the letter in the first place.

(3). Paul expressed hope that this woman will be saved by Christ, even though she is in error.

Verse 15 "she will be saved through (the) childbearing" is a reference to the woman's salvation through the Incarnation of Christ (the childbearing). The word *teknogonia* is used just once in Scripture, and the word is NOT a verb (childbearing)-- it is a noun (THE childbearing).

This is a reference to the Messiah, who was born from a woman despite the deception of Eve. The Messiah came to destroy the destroyer, to crush the head of the Serpent who deceives, and the deceived woman of I Timothy 2 will be saved through "the childbearing" if stops teaching heresy, learns of Christ in complete submissiveness (v. 11), and continues in "faith, love, and holiness in propriety."

(4). Scripture only expresses a prohibition on women teaching error, never on women teaching men.

A similar passage to I Timothy 2:11-15 is Revelation 2:20: "But I have this against you, that you tolerate the woman Jezebel, who calls herself a prophetess, and she teaches and leads My bond- servants astray so that they commit acts of immorality and eat things sacrificed to idols."

The problem with Jezebel was not that she "teaches and leads." The problem with Jezebel was that she taught and led others "astray."

The only solution for a woman who teaches and leads astray is for her to first learn the truth. This is precisely the solution Paul proposes to Timothy for the woman of I Timothy 2. She must first learn "in quietness and full submission" (v.11). By the way, this is also a good practice for any man who is teaching error. He should be confronted and told to FIRST learn in quietness and submission before he attempts to teach.

(5). The people who misinterpret Paul and attempt to prohibit women from teaching or leading men are ignoring the entire tenor and teaching of the New Testament.

God empowers His people through giftings and anoints His people to fulfill their calling through the Holy Spirit. The giftings of God are never distributed according to gender. The calling of God is never limited according to physiology. When the daughters of Philip prophesied, it was by the giftings of God and the anointing of the Spirit. When Anna taught the men in the Temple, it was in fulfillment of the calling of God on her life and through the giftings and anointing of the Spirit. From Priscilla, to Lydia, to Junia, to Phoebe, and to all the rest of the New Testament women God used to expand His kingdom through prophesying, teaching and leading other men and women, God has gifted and anointed as many women as He has men.

Let's not traditions trump truth.

Chapter 20: The Misinterpretation of I Timothy 2:9-15 that Leads to a Belief in Inherent Male Authority

Cultish behavior gives me the heebie-jeebies. A cult is defined as a group of people who follow a particular system of religious behavior established by an authoritative or revered person. Lest someone argue that Christianity is a cult, remember that Jesus said, "You shall know the truth, and the truth shall set you free." Jesus frees people; cult leaders bind people. Jesus speaks truth to people; cult leaders lie to people. Jesus empowers people; cult leaders oppress people. Christianity is not a cult nor is Jesus, a cult leader. He saves His people from systems that bind.

Some Christian men, however, have set themselves up as authorities in the institutional church and implemented systems of control that turn pockets of evangelicalism into cultism. This is what gives me the heebie-jeebies.

The most prominent example of cultism within evangelical Christianity is the system of behavior imposed on women within the ekklessia (assembly) of Christ. Christian women are told by some authoritative church leaders that "women must never teach men; women must be silent in the assembly; women must not have any authority over men, and women should seek to be passive servants to, and receivers of, male leadership, but should never exhibit characteristics of vibrant leadership when males are present."

FRAUDULENT AUTHORITY

This system of behavior for women is cultic; for it is definitely not Christian nor is it consistent with the teachings of Scripture.

The Scriptures and the Freedom of Women

The New Testament gives many examples of women teaching men (cf. Luke 2:25-38; Acts 21:9; John 4:28-29). Women served as *deaconia* in the early church (cf. Romans 16:1-2).

Women were co-laborers with men in Christ's kingdom (cf. Romans 16:3) and at least one of Christ's apostles was a woman (cf. Romans 16:7). Males and females accompanied Jesus throughout His earthly ministry (cf. Luke 8:1-3).

Gifted men and women spread the good news of the kingdom. God first used women to preach (proclaim) the resurrection of His Son (cf. John 20:1-2). Male disciples later proclaimed the resurrected Christ in the same manner female disciples first preached Him (cf. Luke 24:1-11).

Women in the upper room at Pentecost received the same Spirit and the same gifts as men (cf. Acts 1:14-15). God is emphatic that in the days of the New Covenant both males and females will prophesy of Him (cf. Acts 2:17-18).

The Apostle Paul encouraged men and women to teach, to pray and to fully participate in the assembly (cf. I Corinthians 11:4-5 and I Corinthians 14:23-24).

God clearly reveals to us that Christian men and women should serve as they are gifted by the Spirit. Any imposed restrictions on women speaking, teaching, or leading in the assembly of Christ is contrary to the inspired revelation of

FRAUDULENT AUTHORITY

God's word. So if the New Testament teaches that men and women are gifted by the Spirit to do the work of the kingdom, why do some put a system of restrictions on women, a system totally contrary to the overall tenor and explicit teachings of holy Scripture?

Several years ago I was called by the Tulsa Police Department to a home where a young man committed suicide by cutting of his right hand with a pocket knife and bleeding out. We found him dead with his head slumped to his chest and a pool of blood at his feet.

Before the young man died, he laid his pocket knife on the middle of an open Bible with these words underlined: "And if your right hand causes you to sin, cut if off and throw it away. It is better for you to lose one part of your body than for your whole body to be thrown in hell" (Matthew 5:30).

I will never forget the gruesomeness of discovering the young man's right hand in a trash can, nor the words of the lieutenant as he walked around the room muttering under his breath, "Stupid, stupid, stupid." We were later told that the man had struggled for years with pornography and masturbation.

The man took the words of the Bible and obeyed them.

However, there is something mighty stupid about a man who reads Scripture and acts on words without taking time to look at their meaning, particularly when the overall tenor and teaching of Scripture is opposite of the action he is compelled to take!

If anybody ever tells you that women should never teach men, or that women should never be in leadership over men, or that women should be silent around men, then you should mutter under your breath, "Stupid, stupid, stupid."

These people, well intentioned as they may be, are committing spiritual suicide by acting on words of Scripture without looking at their meaning. The system they seek to impose is opposite to the overall tenor and teachings of Scripture on the subject of women. Here are the words some commit spiritual suicide over:

"In like manner also, see that women adorn themselves in modest apparel, with shamefacedness and sobriety; not with braided hair, or gold, or pearls, or costly array; But (which becometh women professing godliness) with good works. Let the woman learn in silence with all subjection. But I suffer not a woman to teach, nor to usurp authority over the man, but to be in silence. For Adam was first formed, then Eve. And Adam was not deceived, but the woman being deceived was in the transgression. Notwithstanding she shall be saved in childbearing if they continue in faith and charity and holiness with sobriety." (**I Timothy 2:9-15**)

I recently had a Christian man paraphrase for me **I Timothy 2:9- 15** and then tell me, "I will never have a woman lead me, teach me, or allow myself to be in a position where women usurp my authority over them because I believe the Bible!"

My friend has the problem of reading words of Scripture and acting on them without taking time to understand their meaning.

Until you understand the problem Timothy faced (the man to whom the words in I Timothy 2:9-15 are written), and until you are familiar with Ephesus (the place where Timothy lived), and until you have a working knowledge of the Amazons (the warrior women that the ancient Greeks believed founded Ephesus), and until you comprehend the influence of the cult of Artemis and the Temple of Artemis which was in Ephesus, the meaning of the Apostle Paul's words will never be rightly understood.

The subjugation of a woman is a system of man's fallen nature.

If the work of Christ involves... breaking the fall, then the implication of His work for the liberation of women is plain." Jesus Christ came to liberate subjugated women. The cultism in evangelicalism regarding women's behaviors will only be broken when people lay aside stupid, false obedience to I Timothy 2:9- 14 and realize the meaning of Paul's words to Timothy.

Ephesus and The Temple of Artemis

Rachelle and I have visited the ancient city of Ephesus, located in modern southwest Turkey. Timothy, the young man to whom Paul wrote (I Timothy), was living and ministering to Christians in Ephesus. At the center of that great ancient city was the Temple of Artemis.

The Artemis Temple was the first religious temple in the world made completely of marble.

The richest man in the world in his day, King Croesus (595- 547 B.C.) of Lydia (modern Turkey), ordered the Temple of Artemis be constructed in honor of the Greek goddess Artemis. Generations of people, even in America, have used the phrase
"Rich as Croesus" to describe wealthy people in their day. King Croesus is given credit by many historians as the inventor of cold and silver coinage. His wealth is legendary,

FRAUDULENT AUTHORITY

and he gave his riches to fund the building of the Temple in Artemis.

Work on the Temple of Artemis began in 550 B.C. and took over a century to complete. King Croesus lived long enough to stuff the foundation of the Temple of Artemis with tens of thousands of gold coins to serve as talismans, ensuring the Temple's protection from destruction.

Croesus was a contemporary of Cyrus the Great, the founder of the Persian Empire. Cyrus was the king who defeated the Babylonians, freeing the Jews from their Babylonian captivity, enabling them to return to Jerusalem to rebuild Solomon's Temple. Therefore, the Temple of Artemis and the Second Temple in Jerusalem (the post-Babylonian exile Temple in Jerusalem) were both built during the same time period (the 6th century B.C.).

However, it was only the Temple of Artemis that became one of the Seven Wonders of the Ancient World because of its stunning beauty. The Temple of Artemis was a temple dedicated to the power, beauty, and strength of women. Marble artisans from all over the world carved Amazon women into the base of the 120 columns. Amazons were "warrior women" from an area north of Ephesus and the Black Sea (modern Ukraine). These Amazon women were known for their fierce fighting ability and had been made famous by the Greek poet Homer in his portrayal of them in The Iliad.

Homer (c. 750 B.C.) also gave tribute in The Iliad to Artemis, the Greek goddess of women and of war. Artemis is called by Homer "Artemis the Hunter, Queen of the Wild Beasts" (Iliad 21.470). Artemis is also presented as the goddess Phosphorous or Light (Strabo, Geo. 1.9.). If worshipped properly and prayed to during childbirth, Artemis promised to deliver women from death while giving birth. For this reason, women in the ancient world revered and worshipped Artemis. Likewise, men worshipped Artemis during times of battle and war.

Since the ancient world was always at war, Artemis was often on the lips of men during times of battle. The Greek men (and later the Romans) prayed to Artemis (the Romans called her Diana), not Apollo in times of battle. In Greek mythology, Zeus fathered the twins Artemis and Apollo through the Titaness Leto. The Artemus cult taught that Artemis was superior to Apollo because she came (was born) born first.

When men and women entered the Temple of Artemis in Ephesus, the women would wear fancy hair braids, bedeck themselves with jewelry and ornate clothes as they prayed to Artemis. Heliodorus said, "Their locks of hairs carry their prayers." There were no sacrifices in this Temple.

The women worshipped Artemis with their clothing, jewelry, and their words. Artemis, in turn, gave them their sexual prowess over men and their deliverance during childbirth. Likewise, men came to Artemis, acknowledging their need of her strength during a time of war.

The men would hold up hands, palms up, just above their waist as they prayed for victory in battle. Not surprisingly Ephesus, above all other places in the ancient world, celebrated the power, strength, and beauty of women and their ability to use their sexual prowess to manipulate and dominate men. The Temple operations, which included prostitution and craftsmen who sold gold and silver idols of Artemis, drove the economy of Ephesus. Hundreds of thousands of people visited the city annually.

FRAUDULENT AUTHORITY

Paul and Timothy's Presence in Ephesus in the Midst of the Artemis Cult

Acts 18:24 through Acts 20:1 records for us that Paul and Timothy spent three years in Ephesus (c. A.D. 55-58), by far the longest time Paul spent in any one city during his three missionary journeys. Paul almost lost his life during a riot in the city because silversmiths who made little statues of the goddess Artemis were upset that Paul and Timothy were cutting into their business by winning converts to Christianity. Paul would later write in I Corinthians 15:32 that he "fought wild beasts at Ephesus."

Did he fight lions, tigers, and bears?

No, the wild beasts were the people of Ephesus who were devoted to Artemis, "The Queen of the Wild Beasts." When Paul left Ephesus in A.D. 58, he traveled south for about 30 miles to the island of Miletus and then called for wise leaders of the church in Ephesus to join him at Miletus where he said to them, "After I leave, savage wolves will come among you and will not spare the flock. Even some among you will arise and distort the truth to draw away disciples after them" (cf. Acts 20:29-30).

Sure enough, less than five years later (A.D. 63) the Christians in Ephesus were in trouble. There were some women or maybe even a single woman, most likely a new convert out of the Artemis cult, who had begun to teach false truth in the assembly at Ephesus. Timothy is sent to Ephesus to help the church and give some correction.

Timothy sends to Paul a letter from Ephesus, giving Paul an update on what is happening and asking some specific questions about how he should proceed (a letter that is not extant). The Apostle Paul sends a response to Timothy, a letter we now call I Timothy. It's important to remember (as we have seen) that nowhere in Scripture does Jesus, Paul or any other apostle restrict women in the assembly. In fact, when a false teacher nicknamed Jezebel begins to have influence among believers in the city of Thyatira, Jesus does not reprimand the church for having a female teacher, but rather He upraids the church for not doing anything about her false teaching (cf. Revelation 2:24).

The Meaning of I Timothy 2:9-15

Now, let's put up I Timothy 2:9-15 again in order to discover the meaning of the words in light of what we know about the Artemis cult in Ephesus:

"In like manner also, see that women adorn themselves in modest apparel, with shamefacedness and sobriety; not with braided hair, or gold, or pearls, or costly array; But (which becometh women professing godliness) with good works. Let the woman learn in silence with all subjection. But I suffer not a woman to teach, nor to usurp authority over the man, but to be in silence. For Adam was first formed, then Eve. And Adam was not deceived, but the woman being deceived was in the transgression. Notwithstanding she shall be saved in childbearing if they continue in faith and charity and holiness with sobriety."(I Timothy 2:9-15)

(1). "Let the women adorn themselves in modest apparel" (v.9).

Obviously, there were women coming to the assembly of Christ in Ephesus similar to the way they used to go to the Temple of Artemis, dressed to kill, with braided hair, gold, pearls, and fine clothing. Paul is letting Timothy know that this mode of dress, particularly in the city of Ephesus, was not conducive to the worship of Christ. What Christ desires is the beauty of goodness toward others, not the drawing attention to oneself in public.

(2). "Let the woman learn in silence with all subjection" (v. 11).

The reason I believe the problem in Ephesus is a particular woman who is in a teaching position within the assembly is that the noun "woman" is in the singular, not the plural. In verses 9 and 10, the word "women" is plural, but in verse 11, Paul switches to "the woman" or possibly "that woman" about whom Timothy had written to Paul.

This silence of women can't be a universal prohibition for all time against all women ever teaching men in the assembly because:

(a). That would violate the tenor and teaching of the rest of Scripture where women frequently taught men, and

(b). Paul has elsewhere encouraged men and women to teach, to pray and to fully participate in the assembly as they are gifted (cf. I Corinthians 11:4-5 and I Corinthians 14:23-24).

Further, the word translated silence is *hesuchia* (quietness). It is used in I Timothy 2:2 to describe what the character of every believer should be, both males and females. It never means "don't speak," but addresses the character of humility. This woman in Ephesus, coming out of a society saturated with the power, strength, abilities and even domination of women through the Artemis cult, needed to realize that she had a great deal to learn about Christ and His kingdom.

(3). "I suffer not a woman to teach, nor to usurp authority over the man, but to be in silence" (v. 12).

This is the key phrase. First, the phrase translated "I suffer not a woman to teach" is literally in the tense of "I am not now permitting a woman to teach." Again, the woman not now permitted to teach is in the singular. It is the same woman of verse 11. This woman needs to learn in quiet humility before she ever presumes to teach because she is still too influenced by Artemis cultic beliefs. This verse can NEVER be used as a proof text for women never teaching men or having "authority" over men.

(a). Deborah gave counsel and taught men and women about the Law of God (cf. Judges 2:16-19; 4:1-5:31). Huldah prophesied to Israel the word of the Lord and led the men of Israel (2 Kings 22:14-20). Priscilla and Aquila explained more perfectly to Apollos the way of God in Ephesus (cf. Acts 18:19- 26). Most importantly, when Jezebel was teaching error to the church in Thyatira, Jesus never once told the church they were wrong for having a woman teach or lead them; He simply said they were wrong for not rejecting her false teaching (Revelation 2:18-29).

(b). "I suffer not a woman .... to usurp authority over the man" (v. 13).

This phrase "usurp authority" translates one Greek word *authentein*. This word is used only one time in all of Scripture-- let me repeat that again--this word *authentein* is used only once in the entire Bible, right here in I Timothy 2:12. This word was used, however, in classical Greek

FRAUDULENT AUTHORITY

literature and it meant "to murder someone." Paul could have chosen nearly fifty Greek words to speak of the ordinary exercise of authority, but he chose a word that more represents someone "dominating, controlling, or subjecting one to harm."

Of course, this is precisely what the Artemis cult taught women to do. Artemis was the female goddess of fertility and war. Women in Ephesus were taught to use their voices, their charm, their sexuality, and their beauty to dominate, control and subjugate men. It seems that this woman in Ephesus was causing trouble in the church by behavior in the assembly of Christ that was way too similar to the ways of the Artemis cult from whence she came.

(4). "For Adam was formed first, then Eve."

Timothy, tell the woman causing problems that her notion she should always have the floor and direct the assembly because she believes women are superior to men--since Artemis came first and Apollo came second--is a misguided belief. The truth is God created man first then He formed Eve from Adam, so it is very appropriate for her, a woman who considers herself a descendent of the Amazons, to sit quietly and learn from those who are older and wiser, even if they are males!

Artemis taught the power of women to dominate men through sexual prowess, but Christ teaches that men are equal to women and there's nothing wrong with a woman learning from others (even men) before she begins to teach men.

(5). "And Adam was not deceived, but the woman being deceived was in the transgression" (v. 14).

FRAUDULENT AUTHORITY

And Timothy, remind her that the Scriptures teach that Eve was deceived. Contrary to what she learned in the Temple of Artemis, males are not always her problem. To be deceived and in need of correction is just as much a possibility for her as it was for Eve. She must move away from her belief in female superiority, a belief reinforced by the Artemis cult.

(6). "Notwithstanding she shall be saved in childbearing, if they continue in faith and charity and holiness with sobriety" (v. 15).

Timothy, tell this woman that she will be okay during childbirth, even if she totally and fully renounces her trust in Artemis. Yes, she lives in a culture that teaches Artemis alone saves a woman from death during childbirth, but the truth is Christ holds the keys of life and death. When women continue in faith, hope, and love--avoiding the sexual immodesty and looseness on display in the Temple of Artemis and the worship of the goddess of fertility and war-- it will be the one true God who delivers them from death during childbirth, not Artemis.

(7). And finally, Timothy, I wrote this letter to help you with the problems in the assembly in honor of "Him who alone has immortality and dwells in unapproachable light, whom no man has ever seen or can see" (I Timothy 6:16).

The people of Ephesus called Artemis the goddess of Light. The men approached Artemis in the Temple with hands raised above their waist praying for victory in battle and in war. Paul reminded Timothy in this same chapter that Christian men should approach Christ in worship with their hands raised and pray for peace with all men, not war. (Timothy 2:5).

Christian women, come before Christ with a sense of modesty and humility, realizing that the ways of Christ are opposite of the ways of Artemis. Paul's entire personal letter to Timothy was an encouragement to him to "fight the wild beasts of Ephesus" and be faithful to the gospel of Jesus Christ and correct the errors brought into the church by "savage wolves" who were remaining under the influence of Artemis theology.

Application:

I recently communication from a female believer in Christ who commented about a previous church experience she and her husband had:

"We spent five years at a church filled with gender role nonsense. It has a way of making women paranoid about their actions, lest they are perceived as being domineering women. One of the church elders took Mr. Hoppy aside one day while at work. He wanted to know about that status of our marriage because I seemed too interested in discussing theology on our church email loop. Women were completely forbidden from speaking in the (very participatory) service, including the one day that all the men except one were at a retreat. (We couldn't even make announcements about the church garage sale.) While women were allowed to discuss theology elsewhere, I guess I must've broken some unspoken rules. I would often be the only women in a group of men standing around discussing theology. Occasionally joining a discussion on the church email loop somehow led this elder into assuming Mr. Hoppy must be very displeased to have such a "domineering wife." He defended me as best he could. By the time we bailed out of that church, yes, the elders were sitting around at lunch with their wives discussing what a "domineering" wife I am."

It is my belief that a lack of understanding of the cult of Artemis is leading western evangelicalism down the road of powerless and ineffective ministry.

Half the body of Christ is refrained from serving and ministering as the Holy Spirit has gifted them because of a mistranslation of I Timothy 2:9-15. Males have taken the role of "spiritual authority," and women are secluded and silenced.

For my part, but the rivers won't run, and the sun won't shine before I let that happen within my small sphere of influence.

Suggestions for Further Study (courtesy Jon Zens)

Linda Belleville, "What the English Translators Aren't Telling You About 1 Tim.2:11-15," Christians for Biblical Equality Conference, Orlando, FL, 2003 (cassette).

Linda Belleville, "Teaching & Usurping Authority: 1 Tim.2:11-15," *Discovering Biblical Equality*, Ronald Pierce & Rebecca Groothuis, eds., IVP, 2005, pp.205-223.

Biblical Illustrator, "Hairstyles of First-Century Asia Minor," 6:4, 1980, pp.71-74.

Del Birkey, *The Fall of Patriarchy: Its Broken Legacy Judged by Jesus & the Apostolic House Church Communities*, Fenestra Books, 2005, 376pp.

Kathleen E. Corley, *Private Women*, Public Meals: Social Conflict in the Synoptic Tradition, Hendrickson, 1993, 217pp. Eldon Jay Epp, *Junia: The First Woman Apostle*, Fortress, 2005, 138pp.

Lauren Fasullo, "What About the Word *Kephale* ('Head') in the New Testament?" and *"A Critique of Wayne Grudem's Understanding of 'Head' in the N.T.,"* 1995. Studies presented to Grace Bible Fellowship, Baton Rouge, LA.

Joy E. Fleming, *Man & Woman in Biblical Unity: Theology from Genesis 2-3*, CBE, 1993, 44pp.

Gordon Fee, "1 Corinthians 7:1-7 Revisited," *Paul & the Corinthians: Studies on a Community in Conflict*, Essays in Honor of Margaret Thrall, Brill, 2003, pp.197-231. Gordon Fee, "The Great Watershed – Intentionality & Particularity/Eternality: 1 Tim.2:8-15 As A Test Case," *Gospel & Spirit: Issues in NT Hermeneutics*, Hendrickson, 2006, pp.52-65.

Matilda J. Gage, *Woman, Church & State*, Persephone Press, 1980, 294pp.

Joseph F. Green, "Diana of the Ephesians," *Sunday School Lesson Illustrator*, 4:4, 1978, pp.34-39.

Rebecca Groothuis, "Leading Him Up the Garden Path: Further Thoughts on 1 Timothy 2:11-15," at CBE International.

Mary Hayter, The New Eve in Christ: The Use & Abuse of the Bible in the Debate About Women in the Church, Eerdmans, 1987, pp.131-133, 148, 155, 161.

Joanne Krupp, Woman: *God's Plan Not Man's Tradition*, Preparing the Way Publishers, 1999, pp.97-107.

Catherine & Richard Kroeger, *"I Suffer Not A Woman"*: Rethinking 1 Timothy 2:11-15 in Light of Ancient Evidence, Baker, 1992, 253pp.

David P. Kuske, "Exegesis of 1 Timothy 2:11-15," at wiseessays.net

Dennie R. MacDonald, *There Is No Male or Female: The Fate of a Dominical Saying in Paul & Gnosticism*, Fortress, 1987, 132pp.

Berkeley Mickelsen, "Who Are the Women in 1 Tim.2:1-15? Parts 1 & 2," *Priscilla Papers*, 2:1, 1988, pp.1-6.

Margaret R. Miles, *Carnal Knowing: Female Nakedness & Religious Meaning in the Christian West*, Vintage, 1991, 254pp.

Craig Morphew, "Thrown to Lions, Woman Pastor Emerges Moral Victor," *St. Paul Pioneer Press Dispatch*, January 30, 1988, p.3B.

Carolyn Osiek, Margaret MacDonald, Janet Tulloch, *A Woman's Place: House Churches in Earliest Christianity*, Fortress, 2005, 354pp.

Alan G. Padgett, "Beginning With the End in 1 Cor.11:2-16," *Priscilla Papers*, 17:3, 2003, pp.17-23.

Philip Payne, "*Authentein* in 1 Timothy 2:12," Evangelical Theological Society Seminar Paper, Atlanta, Ga., November 21, 1986.

Philip Payne, "Women in Church Leadership: 1 Tim.2:11-3:13 Reconsidered," *Japan Harvest*, #4, 1981-82, pp.19-21.

Rena Pederson, *The Lost Apostle: Searching for the Truth About Junia*, Jossey-Boss, 2006, 278pp.

"Professor Made to Leave Seminary 'Because Women Can't Teach Men,'" *Tyler [TX] Morning Telegraph*, January 27, 2007, p.3A.

Cheryl Schatz, "Is There A Law That Forbids Women from Teaching Men?" Women In Ministry Blog, July 2006, at Strive to Enter or mmoutreach.org

"Seven Wonders of the World, Version 2.0," *Duluth News Tribune*, March 19, 2007, pp.A1,A5.

Henry E. Turlington, "Ephesus," *Sunday School Lesson Illustrator*, 4:4, 1978, pp.40-49.

Willard Swartley, "The Bible & Women," *Slavery, Sabbath, War & Women: Case Issues in Biblical Interpretation*, Herald Press, 1983, pp.178-183,324.

Frank Viola, "God's View of a Woman," ptmin.org

Frank Viola, "Now Concerning A Woman's Role in the Church," www.ptmin.org/role.htm

Jon Zens, "Romans 16:1-16 – Brothers & Sisters Doing Kingdom Work," 7th Searching Together Conference, Osceola, WI, 2006 (cassette).

Jon Zens, "Those With the Most Spiritual Influence Live As Those With No Authority," 6th Searching Together Conference, Osceola WI, 2005 (cassette).

Jon Zens with Cliff Bjork, "Women in the Body of Christ: Functioning Priests or 'Silent' Partners?" *Searching Together*, 31:1-3, 2003, 47pp.

Chapter 21: All the Ekklesia Have Voices (Corinthians 14:34-35)

In I Corinthians 14:34-35 the Apostle Paul writes:

"As in all the churches of the saints, the women should keep silent in the churches. For they are not permitted to speak, but they should be subordinate, as even the Law says. If there is anything they desire to know, let them ask their husbands at home. For it is shameful for a woman to speak in church" (I Cor. 14:34-35).

I believe Paul is "quoting" the views of the Judaizers in these two verses, not expressing his own views, in order to correct their false teaching. Judaizers in the Corinthian church sought to bring the synagogue traditions into the Christian assembly. These Judaizers were "zealous for the Law," or the teachings of the Talmud (Acts 21:21), and caused all kinds of problems in the early church. Paul is blunt about them in II Corinthians 11, calling them "false apostles" and "deceitful workers" (II Cor. 11:13), and telling the Christians at Corinth to resist the false practices of the Judaizers and stand firm to the New Covenant "traditions" that Paul had taught them (see I Corinthians 11:2).

Paul taught that all the members of the assembly, both male and female, could participate in congregational worship (see I Cor. 14:31 and 14:39), and it is expected that women in the church will publicly pray and teach just as men publicly pray and teach (see I Corinthians 11:5). The entire discourse of the New Covenant Scriptures is that God's priesthood is composed of males and females, slave and free, Jews and Gentiles. There is no separation of race, nationality, gender or color in the God's New Covenant priesthood. Each of us has been made a priest (Revelation 1:5), and we all form a royal priesthood (I Peter 2:9).

So, the startling prohibition of I Corinthians 14:34-35 seems discordant and unconnected to the rest of the New Covenant Scriptures. There's a reason for this -- it is discordant and unconnected.

Paul is quoting the views of the Judaizers regarding women in I Corinthians 14:34-35. He quotes it in order to correct the Judaizers' false views which were being imposed upon the Christian churches, including the church at Corinth. The Judaizers had been taught four things about the role of women in the synagogues when they were Jews, and they wished to make "the church" conform to these restrictions.

(1). The Jews believed women were not qualified to be learners in the synagogue because the talmudic literature forbad them from learning. Their presence in the synagogue was tolerated, but they were to be unobtrusive and silent, never interferring with the work of the men. The Judaizers wished this tradition to be carried over into all the churches. But Paul argues throughout I Corinthians for the full participation of women within the assembly (see I Corinthians 14:31 and 39).

(2). The Jews recognized that a woman in the synagogue might at some point wish to move from passive attendance to actually learn something in the synagogue, but this was viewed as an exceptional occurance and not the norm. Therefore, on the rare occasion a woman desired to ask a question in order to learn, she was instructed to maintain her silence in the assembly and wait to ask her husband after leaving the synagogue and returning home. The Judaizers

FRAUDULENT AUTHORITY

wished to keep the same passivity of women in the early Christian churches. But Paul expects women to pray and prophesy, the two acts of worship in the assembly, in the same manner, that men pray and prophesy. Women compose half the priesthood (see I Corinthians 11:5).

(3). There is the assumption in the synagogue that all Jewish women would be married; it was even expected by leaders in the synagogue that Jewish women would marry. The Judaizers believed the same thing should be true about all women in the early church. But Paul argues his preference that Christian women remain single for the purpose of ministry (see I Corinthians 7:34).

(4). The Jews believed, and it was reinforced by the Talmud, that only the males should receive religious instruction. Jewish husbands were the source of their wives learning. Women should remain silent within the context of the synagogue. The Judaizers carried this tradition into the early churches and taught just as firmly that all Christian women should be silent in the churches. But Paul has taught that the priesthood of God is composed of both males and females, and there is equality within the priesthood in both role and function (see I Corinthians 11:11 and Galatians 3:28-29)

Paul states the Judaizers beliefs about women in I Corinthians 14:34-35 to only refute it. In other words, the "women keep silent" passage is not God's commandment, but corrupt teaching about to be exposed!

Gilbert Bilezikian writes:

"It is worth noting that in 1 Corinthians more than in any of his other Epistles, Paul uses the é particle to introduce rebuttals to statements preceding it. As a conjunction, é appears in Paul's Epistles in a variety of uses. But the list below points to a predilection for a particular use of é which is characteristic mainly of 1 Corinthians." The verses he listed I also list below, in the order they appear, with a notation indicating the appearance of the é particle, in each case translating it as "Nonsense!" as Bilezikian did to indicate its flavor:1 Cor. 6:1-2-- "If any of you has a dispute with another, dare he take it before the ungodly for judgment instead of before the saints? (é Nonsense!) Do you not know that the saints will judge the world? And if you are to judge the world, are you not competent to judge trivial cases?"

Likewise, in I Corinthians 14:34-35 Paul states a belief that he then refutes using the Greek eta. I Corinthians 14:35 states: "If there is anything they desire to know, let them ask their husbands at home. For it is shameful for a woman to speak in church."

Now, look at I Corinthians 14:36: "What! Did the word of God originate with you, or are you the only ones it has reached?"

The "What" is the Greek eta; the conjunction Bilezikian points out that Paul uses throughout Corinthians to refute false teaching. There are actually two of these eta particles in this text, so Paul is expressing his disbelief (a compounded disbelief) that anyone would think that men only are the mouth pieces of God and that women should be silent in their presence. Paul states his objection to that kind of thinking very clearly.

"Did the word of God come only to you? What! (Note: this "What!" is the second eta in the text) Are you the only one's it has reached?" Paul is utterly refuting the belief that men only can speak in the church.

FRAUDULENT AUTHORITY

A few years ago I taught from this I Corinthians 14:35-36 passage, and as always we had a question and answer time after the study. A woman about seventy years of age who had been a lifelong member of a traditional SBC church in Nevada desired to comment about what I had taught. She was seated next to her husband, and she raised her hand to be recognized and was called upon, she spoke and disagreed quite strongly with my interpretation.

She believed I Corinthians 14:33-35 was a COMMANDMENT FROM GOD and after explaining her reasoning, she concluded emphatically that God wanted women to be silent "in church."

When she was finished I gently suggested that if she believed my interpretation of I Corinthians 11:34-35 was wrong and her interpretation was right, then she should have never raised her hand to be recognized, she should have never voiced her beliefs in the assembly, and she should have waited until she and her husband arrived home before she asked a question of HIM or made a comment to HIM about what I had taught.

That is what the text says!

So either she must believe that what I'm teaching is right and then she is FREE to ask questions of her pastor, at any time, any place, for any reason the assembly is gathered, or she must be true to and consistent with her beliefs and remain absolutely silent in church.

Her response?

She said she was not "in church," so she could speak. Mind you; we were in our Fellowship Hall on Wednesday night with a couple of hundred believers present. There were numerous other small groups from our church meeting throughout our facility and around the city that night. But, in our new member's mind, we were not "in church" that night because we weren't in the "auditorium" and having a typical Sunday morning "church" service.

Her comment led me to to think many Southern Baptists don't have a working, biblical understanding of what the church is. Traditional Southern Baptists often seem more Jewish or Roman Catholic in their views of the assembly (church) and authority (clerics) than the writers of the New Testament.

I believe that the Bible teaches that where two or three are gathered in the name of the Jesus Christ, the assembly is gathered and Christ is at the center of His people.

So Wednesday night is as much church as Sunday morning. Tuesday night small group is as much church as Wednesday night Bible study. Tuesday morning's gathering for fellowship, service, and worship is as much church as Sunday night's discipleship classes.

We, the people, are His church, and when or where we assemble, as few as two or three, His church is convened.

So move over Judaizers; all the people of God, men, and women, are free to function.

Chapter 22: Do You Think of a Building with a Steeple or a Body of People?

When you hear the word "church," do you think of a building with a steeple or a body of people?

"When someone mentions they have a female pastor of their church, I immediately reply that they do not have a pastor and they do not have a church." John MacArthur

"When a pastor declares a female can't pastor a church, I immediately reply every Christian female is the church, and she's more qualified to pastor herself than he is." Wade Burleson

One of the fundamental problems with institutional Christianity today is the mistaken belief by professional pastors that the church of Jesus Christ is similar to the temple of national Israel.

It is often said in the institutional church pulpit that the people are the church, but in practice, the church is seen as the institution.

Even the esteemed John MacArthur makes the mistake of turning the church into an institutional structure like the Old Covenant temple of Israel.

In the Old Covenant, temple leaders were all male. In the Old Covenant, birthright, and gender were everything. In the Old Covenant, a hierarchy of power and authority set apart the priests (all male) from the laymen (males and female). If you were a Jewish, male, temple leader, you were both in theory and in practice closer to God because you were the priest, and only you could abide in the temple.

When Jesus inaugurated the New Covenant on the night before He died, He told His disciples that through the sacrifice of His body and blood He would inaugurate a New Agreement between God and sinners whereby the world (not just Israel), males and females (not just males), all people (not just the priests), could come freely and boldly before God's "throne of grace" through faith in the obedience of God's Son.

The problem of male patriarchy today is a theological one.

John Gill, the pastor of Charles Spurgeon's Metropolitan Tabernacle Church one hundred years before Spurgeon, taught me that in the New Covenant, the ordinances - baptism and the Lord's Supper - are ordinances (or "commandments") of Christ, and not the "church" (e.g., "institutional church"). I will never forget the light bulb that went on in my head when I read this Baptist preacher's writings (from 250 years ago no less!) and discovered that what keeps men believing the church is an institution is the institutional ritual of only "ordaining" men to carry out "the ordinances."

In other words, John MacArthur and others sees "baptism" and the "Lord's Supper" as ordinances of "the church" (e.g. institutional church with a "steeple") and so, any "church" that "ordains" females is not a church, because God never allows "females" to participate in the ordinances - they aren't priests unto God.

Well, I believe Christ commanded baptism and the Lord's Supper, and these two things are not under the "authority" of the institutional churches. So any person in Christ (male or female) may properly and biblically baptize a convert to Christ, and any person in Christ (male or female) may properly and biblically share and serve communion (e.g., bread and wine) with other believers in remembrance of Christ.

Any Christian may do this - because any Christian (male or female) is the church. Christ commissioned His church (e.g. "us") to keep the ordinances of baptism and the Lord's Supper!

So...

I understand when MacArthur speaks of "the church" he's talking about a building with a steeple. When I speak of "the church" I am talking about a body of people.

God gifts His people as He sees fit.

Of course, most of us belong to an institutional church. Some Christians may have "problems" with females in a position of "pastor" at an institutional church, but that "problem" is no different than the problem some men once had with a woman being President of the United States, or CEO of a national corporation, or .... well, you get the picture.

As long as there are those who continue to think of the "church" as an institution like the Old Covenant temple of Israel, then alleged *inherent* male authority would be defended. But when we begin to see the NEW TESTAMENT definition of the church as a body of believers who serve God and each other as He's gifted us (male or female), then we move down the road of true New Covenant living.

Chapter 23: A Word about "Authority" in Marriage

I was recently reading John McArthur's blog *Grace to You* and came across a comment with several questions that I found interesting. I did not see any attempt to answer the lady's questions, so I thought I would respond here at Grace and Truth to You. The woman wrote:

"I am concerned about a marriage situation in which the husband is an OB-GYN doctor. He believes they should not use birth control and delivers all their children at home. She is exhausted with the load of the continual pregnancies and the little ones. He is not willing to allow her to have outside help in the home. She would like to be able to limit the pregnancies.

He rules! She submits.

How does this fit in with God's balance of the man loving the woman? What are her options in this type of marriage? How can she disagree and be biblically correct? Any insights on this? I would love to hear them."

McArthur, Piper and other conservative Bible scholars I admire are fond of referring to the husband's "authority" over his wife. There is only one place in the entire New Testament, however, where the word "authority" (exousia) is used in reference to the husband and wife--I Corinthians 7:4:

FRAUDULENT AUTHORITY

"The wife has not authority (exousia) over her own body, but the husband. In the same manner, the husband has not authority (exousia) over his body, but the wife."

Authority in the marriage seems to be mutual between husband and wife. Paul goes on to affirm mutual authority by saying in the next verse that the sexual union in marriage is an act requiring "mutual consent" or agreement. The Greek word is "symphonou" from which we get our the English word "symphony." In an orchestra, there is harmony in the symphony when all instruments are played at the right time and the right place with mutual understanding and agreement. There is a discordant and disharmonious symphony if even one instrument strikes out on its own against the wishes of the rest.

So it is in marriage. The Bible is quite clear in its answer to the lady's questions above.

(1). There is no sexual union unless both the husband and wife agree.

(2). Multiple childbirths requires mutual consent, not the demands of one.

(3). Disagreement in marriage is not only biblical, but it is also expected, thus the instructions of I Corinthians 7.

(4). The loving spouse will honor the wishes of the one being loved and wait for mutual consent.

(5). Authority and submission, according to the sacred text, is mutual in the husband and wife relationship.

It's ironic to me that many inerrantists seem to want the sacred text to say that which it doesn't. It's time we actually believed the Bible and obeyed it.

Authority in Marriage Should Bring Unity

A word often heard in our evangelical, conservative circles is the English word "authority." Christians are told they must be under the covering of their authority; wives are to be submissive to the authority of their husbands, churches are to obey the authority of their elders, etc...

Without a doubt, believers are under the headship of Christ as their authority, but is the standard, conservative teaching of male authority over females, or a husband's authority over his wife actually biblical?

Most evangelical conservatives claim the husband "has the authority," and the wife is to submit to it.

Again, is that biblical?

The often-quoted book complementarian book *Recovering Biblical Manhood & Womanwood* (1991), devotes entire chapters to passages like Ephesians 5:21-33, 1 Corinthians 11:3- 16. Colossians 3:18-18, and 1 Peter 3:1-7. But the ONLY text in the Bible that actually uses the word "authority" in the context of marriage, 1 Corinthians 7:1-5, is given no consideration.

Likewise, in John Piper's book What's the Difference? Manhood and Womanhood Defined by the Bible (2001) there are two lists of verses dealing with marriage provided, but 1 Corinthians 7:1- 5 is not even included (see pages 21,66).

FRAUDULENT AUTHORITY

Jon Zens, the author who pointed out to me the above facts, has also written me an email with some interesting insight into I Corinthians 7:1-5 and the Bible's use of the word "authority" (Gr. exousia) in connection to marriage.

His conclusions, based on the sacred text itself, may surprise you, but if you truly cherish the teaching of the Bible over man's opinions, they may also change the way you teach on the subject of "authority" within marriage.

First, 1 Cor.7:1-5 is the only place in the NT where the word "authority" (Greek, exousia) is used with reference to marriage. But it is not the authority of the husband over the wife, or vice versa, that is in view, but rather a mutual authority over each other's body. 1 Corinthians 7:4 states that the wife has authority over her husband's body. One would think that this would be a hard pill to swallow for those who see "authority" as resting only in the husband's headship.

Second, Paul states that a couple cannot separate from one another physically unless there is mutual consent (Greek, symphonou). Both parties must agree to the separation, or it doesn't happen. The husband cannot override the wife's differing viewpoint.

John Piper suggests that "mature masculinity accepts the burden of the final say in disagreements between husband and wife, but does not presume to use it in every instance" (p.32). The problem with a dogmatic statement like this is that it will allow for no exceptions. But 1 Corinthians 7:5 contradicts Piper's maxim. If the wife disagrees with physical separation, the husband cannot overrule his wife with the "final choice" (p.33). Such separation can occur only if both husband and wife are in "symphony" (unity) about such an action.

Now if mutual consent applies in an important issue like physical separation from one another for a period of time, wouldn't it seem proper that coming to one-mindedness would be the broad model for decision-making in a healthy marriage? Piper feels that "in a good marriage decision-making is focused on the husband but is not unilateral" (p.32).

Considering 1 Corinthians 7:1-5, I would suggest that decision- making should focus on finding the Lord's mind together. Over the years the good ideas, solutions to problems and answers to dilemmas will flow from both husband and the wife as they seek the Lord as a couple for "symphony."

1 Corinthians 7:5 throws a wrench into the works for those who would include the husband's "final say" in male headship. Paul teaches that unless the couple can agree on a course of action, it cannot be executed.

I suggest that this revelation invites us to re-examine what the husband's headship really entails (cf. Gordon D. Fee, "1 Corinthians 7:1-7 Revisited," Paul & the Corinthians: Studies On A Community in Conflict, Trevor J. Burke/J. Keith Elliott, eds., Brill, 2003, pp.197-213).

Chapter 24: The Divorce Rate and Men Who Have Authority in Marriage

In 2010 the Southern Baptist Convention passed a resolution entitled On the Scandal of Southern Baptist Divorce. The resolution states "that conservative Protestants in the United States of America are divorcing at the same rate, if not at higher rates, than the general population." The resolution further states "the acceleration in rates of divorce in Southern Baptist churches has not come through a shift in theological conviction about scriptural teaching on divorce but rather through cultural accommodation."

Sometimes I am perplexed by the logic of Southern Baptist assemblies. Rather than boycotting Disney World at our business meetings, we might want to consider a corporate course or two in logic. How can the divorce rate in every state in the union be declining while at the same time the Southern Baptist divorce rate is accelerating, but we Southern Baptists are said to be "accommodating culture"? Read again the precise words of the divorce resolution:

"The acceleration in rates of divorce in Southern Baptist churches has not come through a shift in theological conviction about scriptural teaching on divorce but rather through cultural accommodation."

Think. If we Southern Baptists were accommodating culture, we'd see fewer divorces in our churches. Unfortunately, the divorce rate is accelerating among Southern Baptist churches.

FRAUDULENT AUTHORITY

I believe I know the reason. Contrary to the illogical conclusion of the 2010 resolution on divorce, the reason the divorce rate is accelerating within the Southern Baptist Convention is precisely because of a "shift in theological conviction."

The leaders of our Southern Baptist Convention have been strongly promoting a doctrinal error called the Eternal Subordination of the Son. The devastating effects of this doctrine on marriages are far-reaching.

Few Southern Baptists even know what this doctrine is, but when you go to a church led by a Southern Baptist pastor who promotes it, the emphasis of the teaching will be on "the authority of the husband" and "the subordination of the woman to her husband" (just like Jesus is allegedly eternally subordinate to the Father). When the emphasis in any Christian environment (home, church, marriage, etc...) is on authority, a breach in the relationship is ripe.

Here's why.

When Adam and Eve rebelled against their Creator, the radial effects of their sin included an innate desire to dominate and control one another by exerting their control over the other person. The curse causes captives of sin to concentrate on establishing an air of authority and forcing another's complete submission to that authority.

Southern Baptist leaders seem to think that what the Bible calls "the curse" is supposed to be the norm. They think this because they have wrongly come to the conclusion that since Jesus is eternally subordinate to the Father, then women should be subordinate to the male in every relationship. Not so. When the first man (Adam) sought to rule over the first

FRAUDULENT AUTHORITY

woman (Eve), Adam was manifesting the curse, not obeying a command (Genesis 3:16).

Jesus came to reverse the curse. Redemption causes curse-filled people to become grace-filled people. Those who seek to rule over others by exerting authority, when they come to see what Jesus says about life, will turn loose of trying to control other people and will only seek to love and serve, NEVER exerting any alleged authority. Jesus said that "the Gentiles lord over others" and "exert authority," but "it shall not be this way among you" (Matthew 20:24-26).

Southern Baptist Convention leaders are wrongly pushing for men to lord their authority over their wives, and calling on wives to submit to the authority of their husbands because of a belief in and promotion of "the eternal subordination of the Son." I've written about this doctrinal problem among Southern Baptists for years, but I recently came across a brilliant article by Dr. Keith Johnson (Ph.D. Duke), the director of theological development for Campus Crusade for Christ. Johnson's article is called Trinitarian Agency and the Eternal Subordination of the Son: An Augustinian Perspective.

Dr. Johnson's article is long, but in my opinion, it gives a definitive refutation for any claim that the woman is to be subordinate to the man in a marital relationship because the Son is subordinate to the Father. Dr. Johnson's summarizes the critical error of those who hold to the eternal subordination of Jesus to the Father (Paige Patterson, Al Mohler, Danny Akin, Bruce Ware, etc....) when he writes:

Bruce Ware claims that "inherent authority" and "inherent submission" constitute the Father/Son relationship; however, this misreads Augustine. "Authority" and "submission" are not "personal properties" for Augustine. To the contrary, "eternal generation" is what constitutes the Son as Son. Augustine is unequivocal on this point. Ware... rejects eternal generation as the distinguishing property of the Son. In Ware's theology (eternal subordination), "submission" effectively replaces "eternal generation" as the distinguishing property of the Son. Augustine is then read through the lens of this alternative understanding of personal properties.

Someone recently called me "the Barney Fife of pastors." I think he meant it as an insult, but I laughed and received it as a compliment. Everybody can relate to Barney. Mr. Fife knew how to say it simply and make himself understood. Let me put my Barney Fife hat on for a moment and simplify and summarize for Southern Baptist men and women what Dr. Johnson is saying in his article:

(1). Nobody in marriage has any inherent "authority."

Christ has all authority, and He sends His Spirit to live within us, dispenses spiritual gifts for us, and provides loving watch care over us so that we might learn how to love and serve each other.

(2). Submission in a marital relationship is "putting others needs before my own."

The submission and subordination of Jesus Christ to the Father was never about 'greater authority' because Christ had "all authority." Christ put the Father's plans first, submitting Himself to the cross in obedience to the plan of redemption (i.e., "If it is Thy will let this cup pass from me. Nevertheless, Thy will be done").

FRAUDULENT AUTHORITY

Jesus Christ also submitted to us (the church) when He sweated drops of blood in the Garden of Gethsemane and died in our place. Submission is never about 'greater authority,' but rather, it is always about putting the plans, desires, and needs of others first. In marriage, both the husband and the wife are to be mutually submissive to one another (see Ephesians 5:21).

Sometimes what is in the best interest of your partner is to say no! In every decision, your partner's best interest comes first. Don't give up on your marriage until you have sweat blood looking out for your partner.

(3). When we stop trying to control our spouse, and we learn what it means to love and accept him or her the same way Jesus Christ accepts us.

Only then we begin to build a marriage on grace and love instead of domination and control. When that happens, the curse is reversed.

We Southern Baptists do a great many things very well. We do missions well. We perform acts of mercy well. But we are sorry at building marriages. I suggest, for the sake of Christian marriages in our churches, it is time for evangelicals to call out and correct those who advocate the doctrinal error of eternal subordination.

Female Subordination to Male Authority Leads to Dysfunctional Homes and Churches

When I first started blogging in 2005, I was told that the most effective blogs are those that focus on one predominant theme. I focused like a laser beam those first couple of years on the unethical attempt by International Mission Board

FRAUDULENT AUTHORITY

trustees to subvert the Southern Baptist Convention as a whole and impose a doctrinal standard on IMB missionaries that that not only exceeded the Baptist Faith and Message, but by its very existence, breached the ethical boundaries of trusteeship and violated the constitution of the Southern Baptist Convention.

It was during 2005-2008 (the years I served as an IMB trustee) that I began to see the problems we had in the Southern Baptist Convention went far beyond the International Mission Board. Convention leadership (trustee boards) had left their sola Scriptura convictions, and out of the fear of "liberalism," became Fundamentalists-- demanding conformity and agreement on tertiary doctrines that had nothing to do with evangelical cooperation on the mission field. One of those thirdstage doctrines is the role and authority of women.

I saw with my own eyes the unethical, unbiblical, and godless treatment of women in the Southern Baptist Convention and I vowed to do something about it. Do I consider the equality of men and women a first-tier evangelical doctrine?

No; but because the Fundamentalists among us have elevated "the female subordination of women to men" as a litmus test for evangelical orthodoxy, I now focus on their dysfunctional views of male authority and female subordination to help my fellow Bible-believing, conservative, evangelical friends realize the errors being promulgated. Female subordination to male authority is promoted by organizations such as The Council for Biblical Manhood and Womanhood, Together for the Gospel, and The Elephant Room.

I only recently heard that Mark Driscoll has identified "the subordination of women to men" as one of the four key

FRAUDULENT AUTHORITY

building blocks of his *Resurgence Movement*. I have addressed the doctrinal fallacies of the Gender Gospel elsewhere, fallacies that plague both liberal feminism and Fundamentalism.

I'd like to give a few examples of how Bible-believing Christian families, churches, and groups move into dysfunctional, even cultish behavior if female subordination is allowed to be taught and practiced as biblical orthodoxy.

Most people are familiar with the removal of Sheri Klouda as Hebrew professor from Southwestern Theological Seminary by men who hold to female subordination and cringe at the thought of a woman teaching men Hebrew.

What many men and women in conservative, evangelical churches don't realize is that there are Sheri Kloudas everywhere--gifted women who are removed from responsible Christian leadership positions and/or forbidden from speaking publicly, teaching others the Word of God, or otherwise providing spiritual guidance to men because they are women.

This absurd position is totally contrary to the Gospel, anti-Christian in nature, and the opposite of the teachings of Christ and His apostles.

If not stopped, it will plague Christian people with a disease of the soul that is worse than leprosy of the skin. It leads to power- hungry men seeking positions of authority and control, and an almost cultish like god complex. "I am in the image of God. My word is Law. You submit to what I say, and don't dare try to tell me what I should do." This anti-Christ doctrine fleshes itself out in conservative Christian homes and churches in various ways. I will give you three examples.

FRAUDULENT AUTHORITY

A well-known Southern Baptist pastor recently told his congregation that he decided to move his family to a new house this year. The price of the pastor's old home ($375,000) and the price of the pastor's new home ($500,000) were appropriately not revealed to the congregation. However, they are relevant to this story because the pastor previously told his congregation that they were not to buy more expensive homes, but rather God desired them to set aside that extra money and give it to kingdom causes (i.e., the church).

Please don't misunderstand me. I advocate freedom for all pastors and all congregations to do as the Spirit leads; even the purchase of million-dollar-homes if that is what the Spirit leads them to do. What I find incongruous is the promotion of a so- called "radical Christianity" by those are actually averse to living radically themselves. People should realize one of the prominent New Testament principles is freedom and Spirit-led living.

The problem is when pastors place themselves as an *authority over the lives of others to tell them how they are to live*, while at the same time doing the opposite of that they advocate. It's much better to be silent on issues the Bible is silent about.

Anyway, back to the main point. What most people in this pastor's church are not aware of is that the pastor's new home is within ten miles of his old home. Before the move, the pastor's wife insisted that the family should not move. She had several very good and valid reasons. However, the pastor informed his wife, that as the man in the home--"the one with authority"--he would make the decision to move and overrule any objections he heard. He said moving was "the right thing" to do, and submission to his authority was "the right thing" for her to do. So the pastor's family moved.

FRAUDULENT AUTHORITY

I have withheld names, but I do hope the pastor reads this blog and realizes the dysfunctional nature of the argument he had with his wife. Multiply this by hundreds of times in conservative, evangelical homes, and you get a picture of the problems created when Christian men have a warped view of their authority.

A friend named Lamar Wadsworth recently wrote to me and told me about his mother's funeral. He wrote:

"When my mother died, we were not allowed to have her funeral at the Southern Baptist church where she was an active member for over FIFTY years because I had asked two women to read Scripture at the service. So the funeral had to be held at my home church, the Heritage Baptist Church in Cartersville GA. My church honored my Mother like she was one of their own and gave her the homegoing celebration she deserved. The following November, on All Saints Day-- without explanation or comment, my Mother's name was included on the list of members of Heritage Baptist Church who had died in the past year. Bill Leonard said we pulled off the first posthumous transfer of church membership in Baptist history." Can you believe it?

A Southern Baptist Church refuses to allow the funeral of one of the members of their church, a member who faithfully attended and gave to the church for over fifty years because the son of the woman who died wanted two women to read Scripture at his mother's funeral. Again, the church is not being named in this post, but for our purposes, we will call it Ichabod Baptist Church for the glory of God is truly gone from it.

There is now a commentary on the Bible "just for women." Dorothy Patterson and Rhonda Harrington Kelley, professors of "Women's Studies" and "Women's Ministry" at

FRAUDULENT AUTHORITY

Southwestern Theological Seminary and New Orleans Theological Seminary respectively, are the two women who wrote the Bible commentary "for women." On the back cover, the purpose of the commentary is revealed: "The Women's Evangelical Commentary is designed to equip women to face cultural issues regarding femininity and gender."

This is Christianese lingo for "it will help convince all you women that you should teach only women, work only in the home, and find your identity in the man God has given you."

I had dinner with Paige and Dorothy Patterson in their home in Fort Worth a few months ago. I have never written the details about our conversation, nor will I, but what that dinner did for me was to reinforce my decision to focus on calling out the bizarre and unbiblical views of women that are being taught by our seminary Presidents, their wives, and other 'leaders' in the SBC.

If the Spirit of God leads you, women, to never work outside the home and to focus on having as many children as possible while creating a safe environment in your home for your husband and kids, then go for it!

If you are led to the seminary to learn the skills of sewing clothes and folding napkins for a proper Southern home, then more power to you! If you live your life submitting to what you perceive as "the authority" of men, particularly the husband God has given you, then fine! Just don't dare call it biblical. Call it your cultural preference. Why? Because one day when you die, you will not have a man you will call your husband. One day when you die, you will exercise your gifts in God-given creative work. One day when you die your entire identity will be in Christ and no other man. One day when you die, you will be given a new name, a new place to live and a new purpose for eternity-- all based upon who you are as a person-- equal to any man God created.

While you are on earth, I hope you find that the teachings of grace and equality in the Bible prepare you for eternity. But if your cultural preference is to find your identity in a man, then just be honest that you feel safer and more secure in the shadow of man's identity, and if you equate your submission to God to that of a visible, physical man, then just be honest about what you are doing.

Don't call it biblical Christianity.

In fact, it's so unbiblical to Christianity portrayed in the New Testament that it may be people who are as comfortable as you in your cultural preferences will write a Bible just for you.

Chapter 25: A Warning to Those Who Rule Over Others for Material Gain

A common mistake made by evangelical pastors today is to forsake the systematic teaching of Scripture (verse by verse exposition) in favor of topical messages that address the 'felt needs' of the hearers.

For example, pastors begin with what they perceive to be a relevant problem in the lives of their congregation (money, marriage, family, etc...) and then craft a message--or series of messages--around the topic, often using proof texts pulled from their context. Throw in a few humorous and interesting illustrations, and "BAM" - you have a 'relevant' Sunday morning talk., and everyone thinks they've benefited from going to church.

Unfortunately, topical preaching that revolves around felt needs is in danger of producing a generation of people ignorant of the transformative power of God's Word. Preacher talks can be relevant and entertaining without an emphasis on God's Word, but they can never regenerate and enliven. Scripture is the 'seed' that produces life. Any biblical text deliberately lifted from its context turns into a dangerous pretext.

Expository preaching is avoided by some because of the philosophy that effective preaching comes from 'picking and choosing' topics that are most appropriate to a target audience. Many biblical texts, in the thinking of some preachers, are impossible to 'apply.' If you don't pick and choose topics, a practice called 'topical' preaching, then there will be those instances when you come to texts like this one:

FRAUDULENT AUTHORITY

"Now in the fifteenth year of the reign of Tiberius Caesar, when Pontius Pilate was governor of Judea, and Herod was tetrarch of Galilee and his brother Philip was tetrarch of the region of Ituraea and Trachonitis, and Lysanias was tetrarch of Abilene, in the high priesthood of Annas and Caiaphas, the word of God came to John, the son of Zacharias, in the wilderness." (Luke 3:1-2).

Andy Stanley would never preach from this text. Why? Because he states in his book Deep and Wide, "While all Scripture is equally inspired, it's not all equally applicable" (p. 185). For this reason, Andy suggests that Scripture texts like the above should not be taught "in big church" (p. 188). You should pick and choose another text which is more 'applicable' to the Sunday morning hearer.

Andy's teaching approach is becoming more and more common among young pastors. I can understand why. It's more enjoyable for the teacher to prepare topical messages. It's far easier for the hearer to apply a topical message. However, I would like to prove in this post that skipping some texts, and picking and choosing better 'applicable texts,' may inadvertently cause people to miss extraordinary, life transformative truth.

The People Who Most Opposed Christ and His Ministry

Look again at that difficult Luke 3:1-2 passage. The physician Luke is introducing seven political and religious leaders who ruled the people during Jesus' day.

These seven people--two Roman rulers, three Hebrew political leaders, and two Jewish religious leaders--eventually

FRAUDULENT AUTHORITY

became the chief antagonists of Jesus Christ throughout His earthly ministry. If it were not important for us to know them, Luke would have not named them. Let's take a look at them.

(A). The Roman Rulers:

Tiberius was the adopted son and sole heir of Augustus Caesar. He was the emperor of Rome (Caesar) throughout Jesus ministry. He became co-regent of the Roman Empire in AD 12 when his ailing adoptive father (Augustus) became bedridden and could no longer function as emperor. Luke gives the date for the beginning of John the Baptist's ministry as 'the fifteenth year of Tiberius Caesar' (AD 26/27).

Jesus once answered a question about paying taxes to Rome by saying, "Render to Caesar what is Caesar's." The Caesar to whom He referred was this Tiberius in Luke 3. Augustus Caesar was emperor over the Roman empire when Christ was born at Bethlehem. Augustus' son, Tiberius Caesar, was emperor over the Roman empire when Christ was crucified.

The second Roman official named in this text is the infamous Pontius Pilate, governor of Judea. He is the Roman official who presides over the trial and execution of Jesus Christ. The American modern equivalent to Tiberius Caesar would be the President of the United States, and Pontius Pilate would be a state governor.

(B). The Hebrew Political Leaders:

Luke then names three Hebrew political officials who ruled during Jesus' ministry in Judea - Herod, Philip the Tetrarch (Herod's brother), and Lysanias. Who are these three men? They are the 'leaders' of the ethnic Jews in Jesus day. They

FRAUDULENT AUTHORITY

were also the sons and political heirs of Herod the Great, the former 'king of the Jews' who died in 4 BC.

Herod the Great went ballistic when the wise men asked him "Where is He who is born king of the Jews?" because he (Herod the Great) was already king of the Jews.

Herod died shortly after the birth of Jesus Christ. His political kingdom was then divided into regional fourths (Greek: tetrarchys) and distributed among his surviving sons to rule (tetrarchs). Leaders of the Judean tetrarchy mentioned in Luke 3 included Herod (nicknamed Antipas), Philip (often called Philip the Tetrarch), and Lysanias.

These men were powerful among the Jews, but they couldn't do anything without Rome's permission

At the birth of Jesus, we read in Matthew 2 that Herod the Great was 'king of the Jews.' Thirty-three years later when Jesus is crucified, we read in Luke 23 that Herod orders soldiers to beat Christ and take him to Pilate. This 'Herod' at Christ's crucifixion is the Herod mentioned in Luke 3. He is the son of Herod the Great and is sometimes called Herod Antipas. The quarter of the region Herod was given to 'rule' as tetrarch included Galilee, the land where both John and Jesus based their ministries. Herod Antipas is the one who had John the Baptist beheaded.

In the ethnic melting pot, we call the United States, it is difficult to find a modern equivalent to the tetrarchy positions held by Herod, Philip, and Lysanias. The closest equivalent might be those men who rule over individual political parties, major corporations, unions, and other powerful economic, political, and cultural entities within America. These positions aren't the highest authority, for

FRAUDULENT AUTHORITY

they must answer to 'Caesar,' but they have a great deal of influence over a specific category of people. **(C). The Jewish Religious Leaders: Two Wealthy, Powerful Priests.**

The final two men named by Luke in Luke 3:1-3 are religious leaders who served as high priests of Israel. Their names are Annas and Caiaphas. Modern Christians know very little about these two men. Annas was the High Priest over Israel for ten years (AD 6-15), until at the age of 36, he was removed by the Roman governor Guratus, the predecessor to Pontius Pilate.

The other man, Caiaphas, served as high priest over Israel from AD 18 to AD 36, a time period that encompassed all of Jesus adult life and public ministry.

Annas had five sons and one daughter. His daughter married Caiaphas. Interestingly, every one of Annas five sons--as well as his son-in-law Caiaphas--served as the high priest of Israel during Annas' lifetime. Though Caiaphas was the High Priest during the time of Jesus, Luke names both Annas and Caiaphas because Annas was the power behind the high priest of Israel.

It was said that "Annas ruled the religious world," even though his own children were the chief priests of Israel and each had their turn as 'high priest.' It was to Annas that the people first brought Jesus after our Lord's arrest. Only after being questioned by Annas was Jesus sent to Caiaphas for official trial by the Sanhedrin. Modern religious leaders, like Annas, have a tendency to want to control and run things 'behind the scenes.'

Annas and Caiaphas hated everything to do with Christ.

FRAUDULENT AUTHORITY

Caiaphas particularly was the chief antagonist of our Lord. Caiaphas lived in a palatial mansion inside the walls of Jerusalem. He served as President of the Sanhedrin.

If you saw Caiaphas walking around the streets of Jerusalem, he would always have his servants and attendants around him, and he would be dressed in the finest purple and fine linen. He ate the most sumptuous meals, drank the finest wines, always traveled first class, and lived better than the 'common Jew.' The modern equivalent of Caiaphas would be the wealthy religious leaders in America who take a spiritual position of authority and power over the common people of the land.

The Group of Leaders Jesus Condemns

It is striking to discover that Jesus says very little about the corrupt Roman and Judean political leaders of His day. These leaders--men like Tiberius Caesar, Herod Antipas, and Pontius Pilate--were all evil men. Yet, Jesus says very little publicly about any of them. In fact, when questioned about the supreme political leader (Caesar), Jesus simply says "Give back to Caesar what belongs to Caesar." Jesus is also completely silent before Herod during His trial. Instead of railing against Herod's abuse of political power, Jesus says nothing. It seems Jesus had little to say about politics.

Yet, Jesus boldly and soundly condemned Annas and Caiaphas, the 'rich' religious leaders of His day.

Ironic, is it not, that modern evangelical preachers rail against and condemn President Obama, state governmental leaders, the immoral behavior of business and cultural icons, but there is an appalling silence when it comes to religious leaders who become rich off the tithes and offerings of God's people?

Notice the anger and greed of the religiously rich in Jesus' day. The Bible tells us in John 12 that after Jesus raised Lazarus from the dead, Caiaphas and Annas sought to kill Lazarus 'because many people were going away and were believing in Jesus.' These people 'going away' from the religious institutions governed by Annas and Caiaphas did so because they had seen Lazarus, formerly a dead man, walking around regenerated and enlivened by the power of Christ. These people had seen the power of real religion. John the Apostle puts it like this:

"The large crowd of the Jews then learned that He was there; and they came, not for Jesus' sake only, but that they might also see Lazarus, whom He raised from the dead. But the chief priests planned to put Lazarus to death also; because on account of him many of the Jews were going away and were believing in Jesus" (John 12:9-11).

There are many places that Jesus condemns the religiously rich (i.e. 'the chief priests') throughout the New Testament, but the most striking example of his imprecatory words against Caiaphas and Annas is found in a parable that is more than a parable.

The Parable of the Rich Man and Lazarus.

One of the most well-known yet misunderstood parable that Jesus gave is the Parable of the Rich Man and Lazarus in the gospel of Luke (Chapter 16).

"(19). Now there was a rich man, and he habitually dressed in purple and fine linen, joyously living in splendor every day.

FRAUDULENT AUTHORITY

(20) And a poor man named Lazarus was laid at his gate, covered with sores, (21) and longing to be fed with the crumbs which were falling from the rich man's table; besides, even the dogs were coming and licking his sores. (22) Now the poor man died and was carried away by the angels to Abraham's bosom, and the rich man also died and was buried. (23) and in hell, he lifted up his eyes, being in torment, and saw Abraham far away and Lazarus in his bosom. (24) And he cried out and said, 'Father Abraham, have mercy on me, and send Lazarus so that he may dip the tip of his finger in water and cool off my tongue, for I am in agony in this flame.'

(25) But Abraham said, 'Child, remember that during your life you received your good things, and likewise Lazarus bad things; but now he is being comforted here, and you are in agony. (26) And besides all this, between us and you there is a great chasm fixed, so that those who wish to come over from here to you will not be able, and that none may cross over from there to us.' (27) And he said, 'Then I beg you, father, that you send him to my father's house— (28) for I have five brothers—in order that he may warn them, so that they will not also come to this place of torment.' (29) But Abraham said, 'They have Moses and the Prophets; let them hear them.' (30) But he said, 'No, father Abraham, but if someone goes to them from the dead, they will repent!' (31) But he said to him, 'If they do not listen to Moses and the Prophets, they will not be persuaded even if someone rises from the dead.'" (Luke 16:19- 30)

Caiaphas, the High Priest, is the rich man in Jesus parable of "The Rich Man and Lazarus." Caiaphas is the man "who lifted up his eyes in hell." Caiaphas, the equivalent to a modern religious leader who becomes rich through his religious service, is condemned by Jesus Christ. How do we know this to be true?

FRAUDULENT AUTHORITY

1). The rich man wears the robes the color of the high priest (purple and fine linen).

2). The rich man mistreats the poor man named Lazarus (just as Caiaphas sought to kill Lazarus).

3). The rich man asks a messenger to go to his 'father's house' (Annas' house).

4). The rich man had five brothers (Annas had five sons, Caiaphas was his son-in-law and considered his brothers-in-law to be his brothers).

5). The rich man desires a warning to be given to his five brothers about their behavior (all five of Caiaphas' brothers--the sons of Annas--followed him as 'chief priest' of Israel).

6). The rich man is told that they will not believe "even if someone rises from the dead" (just as Caiaphas, his father Annas, and his five brothers refused to believe in Jesus after Lazarus had been raised from the dead).

If you are a topical preacher, you might pick the parable of the
Rich Man and Lazarus and wax eloquent on the subject of 'hell.'
You might say something like

    (1). Hell is real;
    (2). Hell is rough.
    (3). Hell is ready.

Then you might give the following application: "If you don't let go of your riches and willingly give your tithes and offerings to the church, you may find yourself waking up one day in hell, wanting to warn others to 'repent' and let go of their riches. Don't wait until it is too late! Give to the Kingdom of God today by giving your tithes and offerings!"

That, my friend, is the sorry state of evangelical preaching today. It's taking a text (the Rich Man and Lazarus) out of its context (the resurrection of Lazarus and the chief priests desire to kill Lazarus instead of believing on Christ) and turning it into a pretext (the false conclusion that the parable is about a person letting go of his money and giving it to the church).

The lessons of the Parable of the Rich Man and Lazarus are only obtained when you systematically and intentionally learn the Scriptures, take texts in their contexts, and focus on the life transforming truth from God's word. The lessons of the Parable of the Rich Man and Lazarus are:

(1). Any of us who are working in ministry to become rich through our religious service may wake up one day in hell, facing the holy judgment of God.

(2). Instead of railing against the world and our American culture, be it politics, business, Hollywood or some other segment of society, we preachers ought to reserve our harshest words for the religiously rich among us, that is those who become rich through their religious service, and focus more on policing ourselves than we do the world.

(3). We do our Sunday morning crowd a favor when we teach them the Scriptures verse by verse because we prevent them any application from false conclusions and will give the hearer a better appreciation for the words and ministry of Jesus Christ."

FRAUDULENT AUTHORITY

The great problem of Jesus day were religious leaders who controlled and dominated the people for their personal gain. The parable of the Rich Man and Lazarus is a warning today for
any authoritarian religious leader who uses his "position of authority" for personal gain.

Afterword: A Healthy Church

My friend Chuck Andrews, a delightful pastor and teacher, and one whom I've respected for years has given me permission to publish an article he wrote on the subject of authority as an afterword to this book. Chuck summarizes beautifully what the Bible teaches about authority in the church and in the home.

As you read this article, ask yourself the question: "Am I reflecting the principles of New Testament Christianity in my life as I love and serve others, or is there a desire in me to control other people to bring them to do my will or what I want?" -- Read carefully Chuck's closing word on the characteristics of a healthy church.

"In the Old Covenant people were born into their position of priest or king. Their authority was inherent in their person according to their birthright. Prophets were called into their positions of authority, and a stereotypical personality doesn't appear to be a prerequisite to the call. The following may show how historically culture has influenced our thinking in the matter of "authority" in the local church.

"The Divine Right of Kings states that a monarch owes his rule to the will of God, not to the will of his subjects, parliament, the aristocracy or any other competing authority. This doctrine continued with the claim that any attempt to depose a monarch or to restrict his powers ran contrary to the will of God." Wikipedia

A Priest is defined as "One who is designated as authoritative on religious matters. In some churches, especially the

FRAUDULENT AUTHORITY

Anglican Communion, Eastern Orthodox Church, and Roman Catholic Church, the ordained church leader who serves a congregation of believers is called a priest. The priests in these churches administer the sacraments, preach, and care for the needs of their congregations." The American Heritage Dictionary of the English Language, the 4th edition, published by Houghton Mifflin Company

A more evangelical term is Prophet. Defined by the *The American Heritage Dictionary of the English Language*, 4th edition, published by Houghton Mifflin Company as:

> 1). A person who speaks by divine inspiration or as the interpreter through whom the will of a god is expressed.
>
> 2). A person gifted with profound moral insight and exceptional powers of expression.
>
> 3). A predictor; a soothsayer.
>
> 4). The chief spokesperson of a movement or cause.

In most of the SBC pastoral training 've been through and, for that matter and in conversation with pastors, it seems all four definitions of a prophet are blended by pastors. Thus, ministers, see themselves as "those in authority" over people with a special gift to tell people what God says. Pastors believe they owe their rule (kingship) to the will of God, and if anyone questions their authority, that person is to opposed to God.

Though most of us pastors confess to believe to the priesthood of every believer, they see only themselves as ordained, educated, and authorized by God to administer the ordinances, preach, and be the all-around expert on ministry.

FRAUDULENT AUTHORITY

And when they speak, it is as the inspired interpreter of God's word and will, with irrefutable insight (because God told them), and pastors will often refer to their "spiritual authority" from God to convince people that they speak for God and should be obeyed. Pastors are trained to convey they are the professionals.

Rationally, biblically, spiritually, and culturally I would defend the "authority because of position and person" viewpoint because I believed it wholeheartedly. My identity was wrapped up in being a prophet, priest, and king-- contemporarily, culturally, and sometimes compassionately called a pastor. This historical, cultural understanding has found its mate in this combined reproduction of prophet, priest, and king from the relics of Christianity.

There are some truths in this understanding—we do owe everything to the will of God; we do believe in the priesthood of the believer (at least in theory); and preaching is a ministry of inspiration, insight, and public speaking. Also, there is nothing wrong with being trained through education and mentoring. I don't believe there is a problem with being a pastor professionally and doing everything you can to be the best pastor you can be.

Diligently leading is not only commendable but commanded in the scriptures. In Romans 12:8 those who are gifted as leaders are to express that gift "with diligence." "The elders who rule (to lead out in care for) well are to be considered worthy of double honor, especially those who work hard (persistent strenuous labor) at preaching and teaching" (1 Timothy 5:17).

Yet, more often than not, we are seduced by our own egos to swallow, hook-line-and-sinker, the historical, cultural perception of authority. Pastors who are more concerned with authority than leadership use that perception to defend their authoritarian posture.

In word or deed, they say something like, "God has called me, ordained me, and anointed me so don't question my authority.

After all, I have a degree, license, and ordination hanging on the wall." Then they throw in something like "It's very dangerous to do anything against the Lord's anointed."

Their authority and identity are postured in "I am the pastor!"

In support of this seduction, it seems that in today's church growth movement, churches are looking for a savior who will redeem their church from irrelevancy, the next king who will lead them to kingdom growth (more numbers), a priest who will represent them before God, and a prophet who will confidently and effectively tell them God's will for their lives.

We are more than pleased to be that person if we can, and if we can't, we judge ourselves against those who can. What is pragmatically a pastoral health, wealth, and prosperity mindset comes through in our conventions and conferences, then it filters into our churches. Paraded before us are a few men, and fewer women, who are highly acclaimed because they are successful as defined by our culture. Then with all the right verbiage and pragmatic values, we deceive ourselves into believing that if we can look, lead, and lecture like them we too will be successful as defined by our religious culture.

The mindset becomes, God wants all pastors to be dynamic preachers, charismatic personalities, and gifted CEOs. He

FRAUDULENT AUTHORITY

wants all churches to continue numerical growth in attendance, finances, and ministries. If we're not that kind of pastor and if our church is not experiencing that kind of growth then it's because we are not allowing God to develop us into the leader He wants us to be. Antiquity has become relevant in this postmodern cultural phenomenon.

Whether these values are by the Spirit or the flesh, it makes no difference. Visible results are what matters. Today, in this Western culture, it is not uncommon for a local church to be developed and grow around a charismatic (not theologically but personality) pastor.

With the advancement of electronics, these types of pastors can become bigger than life being broadcast to multiple locations and reaching thousands through video and the internet. Accordingly, pastors can begin to judge themselves in comparison to these bigger than life images.

Also, churches can begin to judge their pastors by those they see on the internet, hear on the radio, watch on TV, or read from the Christian bookstore. Unfortunately, lay leaders can be seduced by their own egos to be a part of a "successful" church and become authoritarian toward pastors, too.

With this marriage of past and present, the stage is set for a culturally acceptable form of spiritual abuse. In some circles, it's called "Pastoral Authority." In other circles, it is "Congregational Authority." In my opinion, in all circles, it is an "identity crisis." Both pastors and churches, are getting their identity from culture instead of from Jesus.

In the New Covenant, we are all (re)born equal and called equally. Maybe at Christmas time, we would do well to remember that the one whose birth we celebrate was born Savior, Prophet, Priest, and King. He alone has authority inherent in His Person and Position. He alone rules His kingdom. He alone fulfilled all the roles of the Old Covenant completely and perfectly. He alone absolutely and faultlessly represented God to people and people to God. He alone is the one and only God-Man. If the local church is His, then He is her Authority. As our authority, He is our identity.

There is to be a harmony and melody between pastors and people. Not a blind following due to authoritarian roles but a relationship built on personal knowledge, reputation and giftedness. Eugene Peterson interprets Hebrews 13:7 "Appreciate your pastoral leaders who gave you the Word of God. Take a good look at the way they live, and let their faithfulness instruct you, as well as their truthfulness. There should be a consistency that runs through us all. For Jesus doesn't change—yesterday, today, tomorrow, he's always totally himself."

Then in verse 17, "Be responsive to your pastoral leaders. Listen to their counsel. They are alert to the condition of your lives and work under the strict supervision of God. Contribute to the joy of their leadership, not its drudgery. Why would you want to make things harder for them?"

You see in this interpretation that a relationship between people and pastors <u>is developed</u> through a willingness of each to serve the other. Pastors receive a positive reception, responsiveness, and respect in direct proportion to their willingness to relate their lives to the congregation and employee their gifts in service to the congregation.

Congregations are to give this positive reception, responsiveness, and respect as they, in a <u>relationship</u> with their pastors, observe the identity of Jesus throughout the lives of their pastors. Christ is "seated far above all rule and authority and power and dominion" (Eph. 1:21) and as servants of His, we serve each other in "the fullness of Him who fills all in all" (Eph. 1:23). It is impossible to serve one another as is defined in Hebrews without people and pastor being in a growing relationship with each other.

The basis of this relationship is a recognition that Christ is the Head and each submits to <u>Him</u> and that one is not more "full of Christ" than the other. In fact, maybe it takes "all" to experience the totality of the fullness of Christ since He "fills all in all."

Regardless of the <u>time period</u>, churches don't need another Savior, Prophet, Priest, or King. We need servants who will demonstrate Jesus, regardless of whether those servants are called pastors, elders, deacons, teachers, councils, leaders, committees, or members. May we all find our identity in Christ and learn to live in Christ.

If we do, we will become servants like Christ.

Then pastors and people will not be campaigning for authority but will be serving one another--accepting one another, respecting one another, appreciating one another, knowing one another."

The End

A Request from the Author

If this book has been a help, I would like to hear from you.

You may write to me at istoriaministries@gmail.com or at wwburleson@gmail.com

I'd love to know your story.

Istoria Ministries exists so that people worldwide might come to know Jesus Christ so that His story can become the center of all our stories.

Finally, your help in getting the word out regarding *Fraudulent Authority* is appreciated. Whether through social media, a review on Amazon, or simply word of mouth, anything you can do to spread the word will contribute to increasing awareness of *Fraudulent Authority.*

Made in the USA
Middletown, DE
25 September 2022